Beautiful Within

Mica Paris

Beautiful Within

Finding happiness and confidence in your own skin

**SIMON &
SCHUSTER**

London · New York · Sydney · Toronto

A CBS COMPANY

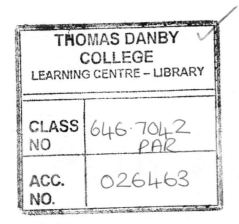
First published in Great Britain by Simon & Schuster UK Ltd, 2007
A CBS COMPANY

1 3 5 7 9 10 8 6 4 2

Simon & Schuster UK Ltd
Africa House
64-78 Kingsway
London WC2B 6AH

www.simonsays.co.uk

Simon & Schuster Australia
Sydney

A CIP catalogue record for this book is available from the British Library

ISBN 13: 978-1-84737-085-3

Designed by Tina Steadman
Illustrations by Liane Payne

Printed and bound in Great Britain by
Mackays of Chatham Ltd

Contents

Acknowledgements

Thanks to the divine spirit for all things.

To my beautiful daughters Monet and Russia Mae who mean everything to me. My mother for being so devoted, for helping me raise my girls and generally being the best mum in the world. My sister Paula for sticking with me through thick and thin. I would also like to thank my grandparents and my dad and the whole family for just being there when I needed them – and still do. It may not always seem so but I do appreciate everything you have all done for me.

Special thanks to my best friend and business partner Stuart Watts. He is the guy who organises my life and expressing gratitude in the acknowledgements is not enough for what he does for me, but it is a start.

Thanks to Brigitte Poole for being such a great listener and friend. Gerry Deveaux for giving me the idea for this book and making it happen. Also to Maria Grachvogel for her wonderful dresses and to Rankin for the amazing photographs on the cover.

And thank you to my editor Angela Herlihy and all the team at Simon and Schuster. It has been great working with you guys. A special thank you to Maria Malone who made the book possible and to Pat Lomax at Bell Lomax Moreton.

There are too many to thank individually but I would like to thank all those who have believed in me and recognized my talent and gave me a chance.

Beautiful Women is a company I have set up to put women in a safer and better place. If you would like further information then please contact stuart@stuartwatts.com

Introduction

Every woman has it in her to create the life she really wants. We can do whatever we like, be anything we choose. All that stops us is that we don't think we can.

There's no secret formula, no magic potion. It's simply about passion and commitment, knowing what you want from life, and being willing to do what it takes to make it happen. It's about believing you can change things when you put your mind to it. Just changing the way you think starts to change the way you feel, the way you look, the way you act, and the way you *are*.

I really think women need all the help and encouragement they can get. We're under attack, bombarded with negative messages about beauty and body image. Celebrities who are anorexics and drug addicts are held up as role models and many real women are under real pressure, battling with self-loathing every day of their lives, feeling ugly and fat and worthless because they don't fit society's distorted idea of beauty. That's why so many are willing to starve to be thin.

Everyone's scared of getting old. Ageing has become a dirty word. Cosmetic surgery is on the up, extreme makeovers are nothing out of the ordinary, and many women are so unhappy with their lives and the way they look they think having operations they don't even need is the answer.

We really are in trouble.

The truth is we all have our doubts and insecurities. We all struggle with the same things: our weight, our relationships, trying to balance work with home life, earning a living, making ends meet, and finding happiness. It's hard sometimes.

We're all looking for ways to make things better. We want to look great, feel confident, and have loving relationships. We want a happy home and a rewarding job. We want the whole package but we don't know how to get it. There *is* a way.

My life has been a real rollercoaster: highs and lows, ups and downs. I've had success and seen it go pear-shaped. I've made money and been bankrupt. I've made mistakes, had setbacks, disappointments, been written off more times than I can remember.

I've fallen for the wrong guy, been betrayed, had my heart broken – not once, but over and over. I've been married and divorced, and now I'm on my own, raising two beautiful daughters, Monet, 15, and Russia, who is 10 months old.

It's taken me a while but, as I write this, at 37 years old, I finally feel I'm getting things right. This book is about my personal journey to a happier life. It's about the experiences that have made me who I am today and the lessons I've learned along the way.

I'm not perfect and I don't claim to have all the answers, but I do know I've finally found a lifestyle that works for me. I'm healthier and in better shape than I've ever been. I'm confident and fulfilled, making a living doing the things I love. And I look younger than I did 10 years ago.

All the stuff I went through – the stuff every woman goes through – was about finding out where I was going wrong and what to do to create the life I really wanted. I've learned there's no such thing as a quick fix and that changing your life means making changes *for* life; that's what gets results.

We're *all* unique, we're *all* beautiful, and we *all* have the potential to do great things. It's just that most of the time that's not what we're told and it's not what we tell ourselves. What I hope this book will do is give you the encouragement you need to tap into what you've got inside already, work out what your dreams are – and make them real.

These last few years I've found out who I really am, what I want from life, and how to get it. Every woman can do the same.

April, 2007.

Wake-Up Call

1

When I was 17, I was signed up to Island Records for my first album.

It was an exciting time for me, a kid from south London, suddenly being given the opportunity to expose my music to a worldwide audience. That album, *So Good*, was a huge hit and my career really took off. Being young and innocent, I was persuaded by the record company to keep up the ideal image, which meant being thin, but my weight fluctuated over the years.

After a decade of success, my *Black Angel* album came out in 1999. I had a massive afro and I was thin – really thin – hollow cheeks, no spare flesh anywhere – I looked more like a model than a singer. People kept telling me I looked amazing so I kept it up, getting by on coffee and cigarettes, hardly eating, feeling like crap. My nerves were jangling but I thought it was worth it if that meant I could fit into a size 10 skirt. From the outside looking in I had it all going on, but underneath I was a mess; my life was starting to implode and being skinny wasn't going to save me.

I loved *Black Angel*, but the release date kept being pushed further and further back. I was committed to the album, but I got the feeling no one else was and, when it finally came out, it wasn't promoted the way I wanted and it wasn't the hit I'd hoped for.

I lost my deal with EMI and, suddenly, I was 30 years old, on my own, a single mum with a young child, no money coming in, not knowing how I was going to make ends meet. The people who'd been around when I was making the album disappeared. It was a case of when you're hot, great, and when you're not, bye. Then, while I was on the floor, three people close to me ripped me off financially and it tipped me over the edge.

One morning I woke up and my heart was thumping in my chest; I had these palpitations that wouldn't stop. I couldn't get my breath and was gasping and wheezing, in a total panic. I thought I was going to die. By the time the doctor came I was really losing it, just about ready to throw myself off the balcony, anything to get some relief. He gave me a shot, calmed me down, and for the next couple of weeks I stayed in bed, crying, falling apart. I couldn't eat, couldn't think, couldn't talk, couldn't do a thing. My body was saying enough is enough. I was having a breakdown.

That was the start of things going bad. I got involved with a guy who was an opportunist and even though I could see it, I still fell for him. He was stunning, with this cute all-American preppy look that I loved. The fact he was aloof and mysterious should have sent alarm bells ringing, but all it did was make me more curious about what was going on inside his head. I was totally taken in.

He moved in with me and we spent six months together with him playing his weird game of emotional catch-me-if-you-can. He was distant and controlling, only allowing me to be intimate with him when he felt like it, but I didn't care: I loved him. I loved him so much I couldn't even eat.

Then one day I started feeling like I wasn't a nice person, like I wasn't attractive or good enough, and suddenly something just fell into place. I started to see that he had issues with self-worth and that I was starting to take on his problems and feel the way he did about himself.

I felt like rubbish, ugly, really crap, and I thought, 'Hang on, I never feel like this about myself. This guy has the power to make me feel really bad.'

That's when I knew he had to go so I made him pack his stuff and I drove him to the airport.

He kept in touch for a while, calling me from France, where he was living. It was only later I found out – by chance – he had a girlfriend there and they had a child. That's when I hung up on him for good. He was toxic and it doesn't pay to have people like that in your life, but that whole experience was devastating, a really painful one.

Believe me, when a guy's being aloof it doesn't mean he's mysterious – it means he's hiding something, up to no good. Aloof translates as bullshit, not that I knew it back then. We can all get sucked in by that stuff, but it's hard to spot when you're in love.

I got really depressed and didn't feel like going out and seeing people. I didn't want my daughter, Monet, to see me like that – a miserable mummy – so my mum took her for a couple of months.

There I was, really thin and glamorous, looking the part, just perfect, but was my life good? No. Was I happy? No. Was everything going well? No. I was miserable as shit: couldn't eat, couldn't love, couldn't have love, couldn't do jack shit, but I looked great.

I can tell you that being thin, that thing so many women crave and see as the answer to everything, doesn't make you happy. You can starve yourself all you like, see your weight go up and down for the rest of your life, feel like a failure when you're not stick-thin, but you're wasting your time. I know because I've been there and done it.

I looked like a model but I didn't know how I was going to pay the rent. I'd come into the music industry at a time when money was being thrown at artists. I was a working-class girl from Lewisham and suddenly I was being given £50,000 here, £50,000 there, the kind of money I'd never seen in my life. The first thing I did was buy a flat and a car – the most expensive BMW I could get my hands on – then I went shopping and bought loads of expensive clothes.

I had no idea how to manage my money and no one ever tried to stop me spending. As long as you're doing well and everyone is enjoying it with you, that's okay. When it runs out they're gone and you're on your own.

I was being excessive, relying on the next advance, living a life that was unbelievable, totally rock star, which doesn't work when you're no longer having hit records.

Before long I had no money, couldn't pay the rent, and the bailiffs were knocking on the door. It was a terrible time and I realised I couldn't go on like that. I had to get my act together. It was the wake-up call I needed.

Catalyst for Change

A lot of us need some kind of catalyst for change: a relationship breaking down, losing a job, being broke, a health scare, the death of someone we love. That's when you wake up and really think about what's going on in your life and what you can do to make it better.

The problem is we all love the familiar and habitual stuff in our lives. We like feeling safe, having things around us we're comfortable with, living in an area we know, mixing with the same people, taking the same route to work, doing the same old stuff every day.

Change can be scary, but it's through change that great things happen. You might not think so when your world's being turned on its head, but it's turmoil that makes you get up and *do* something. You're never going to change your life sitting in front of the telly night after night. It's when things go pear-shaped that you can turn things around. When life gives you that kick it's an opportunity, and it's up to you to wake up.

Those really devastating wake-up calls we all get from time to time make us think about life in a different light and question what we're doing here, and our purpose.

> Change can be scary, but it's through change that great things happen

Being Conscious Takes Work

After my breakdown a few years ago I started to change my life. I didn't want to operate on auto-pilot, let things drift, so I got busy creating the life I really wanted. That meant being conscious. The moment you become conscious things start to change. It's as important as all the other things you do, like eating well and exercising, to take care of yourself.

I'm on a journey, focused on where I want to go and what I want to achieve, aware that change takes time. I've spent the last seven years or so working on myself, not always getting it right, sometimes feeling like I'm not getting anywhere, but, it doesn't matter what happens, I stick at it.

I absolutely believe that if you want to succeed you need to wake up and do some serious work on yourself. You need to become more self-aware, think about the kind of person you are and how you live your life, make a conscious effort to change.

We all slip, that's what being human means, but you have to get busy again, and be consistent, because the work on yourself doesn't stop. Being conscious is a job for life; it takes effort. Some people don't want to work, they'd rather ignore life's wake-up calls and go back to sleep, and that's okay. We all have a choice.

All I can say is that the other way, the *un*-conscious way, doesn't bring fulfilment. No one can give you the life you want. *You* have to do it yourself. It's about taking responsibility, being the creator of your own destiny, and it's a massive job.

Think of life as your own personal movie. You star in it, write the script, direct the action, choose the rest of the cast, and decide how the whole thing's going to play out. If you don't like the movie you're in you can stop it, sack the director, start again. Every one of us has that power, but often we're frightened to use it.

Just think how amazing it is, though, to be able to make the life you want. It's not some impossible dream I'm talking about; this is what all of us can do – *if* we choose to.

What I'm saying is, you don't have to be debilitated by your situation. You don't have to believe that's all there is. I don't care how bad you feel or how bad things look, you *can* change it.

The Power of Emotions

I had a very bad day recently, went into a complete funk over my ex, Andreas, the father of my youngest daughter, Russia. He's now with someone else, living in Italy, but we see him and he spends time with his child. I got home after he'd visited and my mum told me he'd been saying how he could get great Italian baby clothes for Russia. That was all it took to send me straight into a deep depression. It was like it suddenly hit me he'd *really gone*, that he had a life somewhere else. It was as if I hadn't taken it in until that moment. I went into this whole thing of how I never thought he'd go, never thought we'd end, all the while feeling worthless and just not good enough. It was all there, a big, black depression.

This went on for hours. I cried. I prayed. I was on the floor. Then I started to think about the good stuff in my life. I thought, 'I'm a good mother, I've got a radio show, a TV series, I make great records, I'm not bad on the eye,' and that's when I started to climb out of it.

The thing is, *nothing* had actually happened, *nothing* had changed, but I'd let a few words send me into a depression and stir up all those painful feelings. That's something all of us do because we're fragile and our emotions give us a hard time if we don't keep them in check. You mustn't allow your emotional state to dictate your life. Emotions *will* dominate you if you let them. They're always going to be there but when you learn to manage them and stop them taking over you've really won the battle.

We've all done it. You're having a good day, one bad thing comes up, you get annoyed about it and it's all you can think about. Suddenly you're not having a good day anymore, you're in a bad way, wanting to know why that bad thing happened. You're thinking about your ex, upset all over again about what went on between you, or angry about the job you didn't get, or something someone said to you. It all comes back and threatens to drag you under.

> You mustn't allow your emotional state to dictate your life. Emotions *will* dominate you if you let them

Don't be hard on yourself. We're only human and stuff *will* come up. Just don't allow it to take over. Replace it. Think about something else.

Victim or Victor?

I was watching a documentary about apes and behaviour that showed what happened when two apes – one well-behaved, the other cantankerous – were put together. Within a few days they were freaking out, beating each other up, both of them cantankerous. The bad one had dragged down the good one, and that's exactly what happens with people.

That's why when you're working on yourself, trying to get your life in order, you can't have people in your life who are bad for you, because I guarantee you'll end up like them.

All it takes is one bad egg to spoil the omelette, one rotten apple to ruin the rest. When you put a positive and negative charge together; positive becomes negative. The same law applies all the way through the universe.

What happens if you're trying to break an addiction – drink, drugs, whatever? The first thing you're told is to lose the people around you who have the same bad habit because all they're going to do is try to make you go right back to the thing you're trying to avoid.

Often we know when someone is not good for us, but we're frightened to do anything about it. What you have to understand is that dropping the negative people makes positive change possible. Negative stuff is like a wall blocking your way. A lot of us have someone standing in the way of us doing the things we want with our lives. You have to make a choice: do you clear that blockage and trust that what lies around the corner is good or do you just carry on and never find out what might have been? I'm not saying it's easy. When I dropped my unsupportive friends to get the singing career I wanted, there was a moment of

All it takes is one bad egg to spoil the omelette, one rotten apple to ruin the rest absolute fear when I wondered if I'd done the right thing. I thought, 'I've just got rid of everybody, I'm totally alone, and I'm terrified.'

That's why the darkest moment is always before the dawn. When I lost everything a few years back and had the bailiffs banging on the door I had no idea how I was going to manage. I was on my own, I was broke, and I was feeling so low I couldn't see a way out. I knew I had to find a cheaper place to live, but I didn't have the deposit. Normally I'd never ask anyone for anything, I'm just too proud, but I had a friend, someone I hadn't known for very long, who was wealthy, and I thought he wouldn't mind, so I asked and he loaned me the money. He had literally come into my life just a few weeks earlier, yet he was happy to help me out and a few months later I was able to pay him back. He came along just when I needed him and I don't think it was anything to do with luck or coincidence or whatever else you might like to call it.

I call it being blessed because that kind of thing happens to me all the time and I think it's because I love people, I treat them with respect, and my whole aim is about wanting to do good in the world. I think when you've got that as your mindset the universe takes care of you and something always turns up when you need it.

What's it All About?

I have this desire in my heart to make a difference, to do my bit to change the world, even if it's just a little corner somewhere. I believe we all have something we're meant to do, that we've been put here to fulfil our destiny. And I believe we can all make a difference if we put our minds to it.

I don't see myself as a blip on the planet. I don't see anyone like that.

I think every one of us has the potential to do something amazing. I want to touch people – make great music, help women see they have their own unique beauty, encourage women to develop a strong sense of self-belief. I get such a buzz from helping people, making them believe in their potential. I really think that's what I'm here to do, but it's taken me a while to work it out.

For most of my life I've been on a mission to rescue the men I've been involved with, and half the time I didn't even know I was doing it. I've allowed one opportunist after another into my life and done what a lot of women tend to do – over-give. What I wanted to do was empower them, bring out the best in them, but it didn't work.

A few years ago, I met a guy at a party who turned out to be a video director. We started seeing each other and I really fell for him. I'd never heard of any of the artists he'd worked with, but in no time at all I was opening doors for him, introducing him to friends in the industry, recommending him, lending him my car for shoots. He did really well and his career went into overdrive.

And, you know what – the minute the success started coming he began to act like I was invisible. I walked into a restaurant one day and there was some girl sitting on his knee. That's when I realised he was with me for what he could get. It wasn't about love, it was about opportunity.

When I walked away I felt used, like it was my music business connections he wanted, not me. It wasn't the first or the last time I've gone out of my way for someone and got hurt. My mum finally got me to see what was going on, that I had a gift for helping people, but I was throwing it away time and again on the wrong ones.

I'm hoping I've finally learned my lesson and worked out that fixing broken men was not what I was put on this earth to do. I don't think it's guys I'm meant to be helping – it's women.

We all have a destiny to fulfil and once you know what your purpose in life is everything starts to change. You might not have worked out where you're going yet, but there's definitely a path you're meant to take. Right now, you probably don't even know half the things you're capable of, but when you're open to new opportunities you'll find they start to come along.

I thought I was just a singer, but now I've got about five different careers and I'm loving it. I can't sit back and take it easy because there's too much to do. I've got dreams and I want to make them happen. We all do.

Once you know what you're here for and you have a goal, something to focus on, you feel different about life. When you have a vision, a sense of what you want to do with your life, you become less self-obsessed and more aware of what's going on in the world around you.

The selfish way doesn't work. Selfish people end up miserable and deprived and lonely. But when you're out there doing your best, treating people with absolute respect, you find you get help from places you'd never dream of. The phone might ring and someone you haven't heard from in ages will be there to give you just the lift you need. It pays to be nice to the people around you – and to yourself as well.

Be Good to Yourself

I was born in England, but my roots are in the Caribbean and I love the way women there really look after themselves and look major. In Jamaica you'll see women walking round with their rollers in all day so when they go out at night their hair is done, done, done. They do their face, their clothes are banging. Caribbean women want to look sexy, be their best. Those women know how to look good and they love dressing up. My mum's like that, always got her nails done, her hair done; she looks good all the time and that's how I was brought up. It's not about being obsessive and vain; it's about taking a pride in the way you look.

When I was living in the States the women there were really big on grooming as well, having manicures, getting their hair done once a week. They always looked that bit more glamorous than women in the UK.

I meet loads of women here and mostly they don't embrace that thing of making the best of themselves, being good to themselves. It's not that they're not beautiful, but there seems to be a fear of looking nice, almost that it's wrong to make the most of yourself. I think it's to do with the British mentality of not showing off, knowing your place. I just don't get that. Why would anyone want to be a shrinking violet? Women tell me they don't bother because they don't think anyone is going to be interested. Well, if you've already made up your mind to be ignored you will be.

Change the movie. Give yourself the lead, the main role, the one that's going to turn heads. We are *all* stars. Every woman has it in her – regardless of how you think you look – it's a case of bringing it to the surface. You don't need to be obsessive, just *groomed*. When you get into a routine of having a bit of pampering, making the most of yourself, you'll realise you can look great. And even if you're not convinced to begin with, it doesn't matter. Fake it until you make it.

My ritual means going to the gym three times a week, working out, having a steam, getting my hair done once a week, having my nails done every couple of weeks. When I've had that time to myself and been pampered I feel incredible, a million dollars. Even if you don't have a lot of time or money, there are lots of ways to treat yourself. At home when I have a bath I use essential oils, lavender or geranium, for relaxation. I burn oils to give the place a good energy, different oils depending on how I feel, and they really work. When I walk into a room and the scent of lavender hits me it's wicked. You've got to do all that stuff. It's maintenance.

Just think what happens when a house is left empty and no one takes care of it – it starts to decay. Same with the garden – you don't tend it, you get weeds. We're no different. If I can't get to the gym and I don't make time for myself I feel like rubbish. The trouble is a lot of women feel guilty about putting aside that time or spending money on stuff like having their nails done. When you've got low self-esteem, how in God's name can you justify splashing out on a spa treatment? You don't think you're worth it, but you are.

When you treat yourself, take care of your body, have that time out, you start feeling good and that filters through to every bit of your life. You're happier so you're in a better frame of mind at home, less likely to lose your temper with the kids. So, what would you prefer – to go without and end up stressed and irritable, or indulge yourself and get that nice calm, chilled vibe?

Just try it, have a treatment, do something special, once a week for a couple of weeks, see how you feel. I really believe it's important for women. We love it. We need it. We want to look adorable and if we neglect ourselves it messes us up and leads to self-loathing.

When you invest in yourself, whether it's a relaxing bath with essential oils, a manicure, having your hair done, whatever it is, deciding you're worth a bit of time and money, does wonders for your self-esteem.

You'll start to feel better and you'll look different. You can transform yourself and you really don't need plastic surgery.

A few months ago I got in a cab and the driver thought I was 25. The reason I look better now than I did 10 years ago is down to the simple lifestyle changes I've made: being conscious of what I'm eating, caring for my body, making sure I drink my two litres of water a day, shedding emotional baggage.

A few years back, I wasn't looking good. I looked hideous. I was eating all the wrong stuff, had put on lots of weight and was absolutely miserable. Now, emotionally, I'm travelling light, and I look years younger for it.

People are terrified of ageing. No one wants to get old. Women are going to extremes to stay young-looking – having surgery, Botox, stuff pumped into their lips. You don't have to do any of that. What makes people look old is worry, stress, inertia, fear. What keeps people young is fulfilling their potential, doing the things they're passionate about, creating the life they want, staying active. Your mind and body are connected and when you're mentally engaged, busy doing great things, it shows in your face. That's the best way of turning back the clock.

What I've Learned

- You can create the life you want
- Being thin doesn't make you happy
- Take pride in how you look – make time for yourself
- We are all stars

Who Says the Grass is Greener?

By the time I was 20 I was living in New York.

I had the most amazing apartment, massive rooms, high ceilings, in a really cool building in Manhattan. My neighbour upstairs was the model Margaux Hemingway. I'd go home, look around the huge reception room with its views over the Hudson River, and think it was about as far from growing up in Lewisham as you could get. I'd come a long way fast.

I was only a teenager and incredibly green when I signed to Island Records. I knew I could sing and the kind of music I wanted to make, but that was about it. I'd only just left Lewisham Girls' School and suddenly I was hanging out with people like Courtney Pine and Bono, working on my first album, as part of the Island 'family'.

I went from being Michelle Wallen to Mica Paris, pop star, with my own flat. When the first album, *So Good*, went platinum my life was in overdrive. I was all over the magazines, selling records like flipping hot cakes. It was all I'd ever wanted. Wasn't it?

All the time I had this nagging doubt in the back of my mind that something was missing, but I wasn't sure what. Singing, being successful, was my dream and I'd made it, but it was as if I wasn't getting the buzz I'd expected. I kept thinking, 'Is this it?' It wasn't that I was ungrateful, it was just I didn't feel fulfilled in the way I thought I would and that bothered me.

My career was going great but my personal life was a bit of a disaster. Just as I was getting some success, my first boyfriend cheated on me with someone I thought was my friend. I was totally devastated. That was my first experience of being in love and having my heart broken. It was so painful. He probably doesn't even know it, but that first album was all about him.

Then I fell for the A & R man who'd signed me and was a huge influence. He 'got' me the minute he met me; he could see the vision I had and he believed in me, even though I was just a kid.

When I told him it was my dream to make a record that would stand the test of time, he didn't laugh. He went with it. I started to fall for him, but I was getting mixed messages back, and I couldn't work out how he felt.

We'd spend all our time together and he really took care of me. Being naive, I thought it was because I was special to him, and I was, but only as an artist. I was a hot new product. While I was falling in love, he was just doing his job and, even though he knew how I felt, nothing ever happened between us.

So, I had a hit album and I was really going places, but inside I was miserable. There was no let-up, it was all rushing about, promoting records, interviews here, there and everywhere, *Top of the Pops* one night, *Wogan* the next. I did every TV show there was. If I stepped off a plane I'd be photographed, and wherever I went people would come up wanting autographs. It was absolutely amazing.

I had all the fame and fortune anyone could ever want, but I still wasn't sure how I felt about it. What I loved, really loved, was singing and performing. It wasn't what I call 'the lights' that did it for me. I wasn't impressed by fame and being famous wasn't what I craved. More than anything else, I wanted to touch people with my music.

It didn't matter how many records I sold I kept thinking I wasn't doing enough, and I kept pushing myself, trying to do more, wanting to find that missing 'something'.

I felt I'd cracked it in the UK, that people knew me and liked what I was doing enough to go out and buy my records, so I went to New York, partly to get away from the heartache of being around my A&R man, and partly to look for another challenge.

I spent nearly two years in the States and had the most amazing time. Suddenly I was on *The David Letterman Show*. I was meeting people like Aretha Franklin and Roberta Flack. I toured with Ashford and Simpson and, the night I opened for them at Radio City in New York, I came off stage, dripping in sweat, to find one of my all-time heroes, Luther Vandross, waiting for me in the wings.

I was working on my second album, *Contribution*, travelling around New York in a limo, living the most incredible life, and I still had that hollow feeling inside. Nothing would make it go away. The bottom line was I missed London. I missed my family and friends. They all thought I was living the dream – and I was – but I couldn't help thinking about my old mates hanging out at the Africa Centre with Jazzie B, having fun, and wishing I was part of it.

I had the highs of performing and the lows of coming back to my apartment alone. I'd shut the door behind me and think, now what? I'd spend hours on the phone to my mum and my sister, Paula, feeling homesick, but not owning up to it.

I was having so much success, but I wasn't having fun. I'd always thought the two went hand in hand, but I was learning a big lesson that fame, money, material things, don't necessarily add up to being happy.

I wasn't getting any love. I was lonely. I'd been brought up in my grandparents' house with loads of family around and I wasn't used to being on my own. And I was starting to feel like the people around me, my new 'family' in the music business, were weird. The whole scene was awash with drugs, and even though I wasn't taking any, I was starting to feel paranoid anyway.

I'd been pretty much thrown in at the deep end and I'm not sure I knew what I was letting myself in for. People kept telling me the music industry was a nightmare, the worst business in the world, but I wanted it so bad I didn't care if it was dangerous. I thought I'd be fine, I'd cope, and I did, but I hadn't realised just how dark a place it is.

It's a tough business with everyone making out they love you when what they really love is your talent. It's not *you* they want to be with, it's the fame and the lights and the money around you. I was so young and so naive, I didn't see it.

When I left New York I was desperate to get away from all the madness. I remember getting back to London and still having that feeling of being alone. I'd been working flat out for years, on the road, living out of a suitcase half the time, and I just wanted someone to come home to, someone special to share my life with. I'd stopped enjoying what I was doing. Everyone around me was partying all the time, getting smashed, and I was sick and tired of it. I didn't like where it was going. I'd really had enough.

I felt as if I'd peaked, like I couldn't go any further. I was afraid the fame and the success would suck me in and send me mad if I wasn't careful. I needed to take a step back and have something real: a normal life. That meant getting married and having a family of my own.

Marriage and Motherhood

I met Michael when I got back from New York. He was a normal guy, Tottenham supporter, the brother of a friend of mine. He couldn't care less about the lights, and I loved him for it.

I'd had so much madness around me, so many fakes, and Michael was real. I'd felt like I was everybody's piece of something, but I wasn't anything to me, like my real world was missing and I was desperate to get it back. I just wanted to fall in love and Michael was a different kind of love for me, an escape from all the other crazy stuff.

I got pregnant really quickly and we decided to get married. Looking back, I was in too much of a hurry, desperate to put together a makeshift family and get back some normality. Marriage was about filling the void in my life. Basically, I was looking for a quick-fix and I didn't think things through, just rushed into it.

On May 18th, 1991, five months after we got married, Monet was born. Motherhood is an amazing thing. I was really healthy when I was pregnant, loved it, loved the way my body changed, and the way I kept wanting to eat weird stuff. I had a thing about Häagen-Dazs ice cream, and Michael, bless him, was brilliant. If I wanted a tub at four in the morning he'd go and get it for me. I had other strange cravings, too. One day I cooked Caribbean chicken and dipped sponge cake, which I never normally eat anyway, in the gravy. It was about the freakiest thing I did.

One thing about being pregnant was that I had this strange almost sixth sense that meant I was suddenly seeing things for what they were. It opened my eyes to all the hangers-on I'd thought were my best friends. For years I'd been thinking everyone liked me because I was a nice person. I didn't think it was anything to do with the fame or having a top five album. Then, when I was pregnant, it was like the veil was taken away and, for the first time, I started seeing stuff the way it really was. Everybody had to go.

I was so happy when Monet came into the world. There I was, looking like crap, with this little thing clinging to me for dear life. It was the first time I'd felt pure, unconditional love, and I was euphoric. She was just what I needed.

For the first time in ages I was happy. I had my own little family.

That was my dream, the three of us in our beautiful house, happy together. That's where my head was and I was desperate for it to work out, but the odds were against us.

Me and Michael were such different people; I was always raring to go, ambitious, a total workaholic, and he was laid-back, happy to just hang out. I'd got my fairytale, but I was the only one pulling out the stops to make it happen. One day I looked at him and I could see the kind of life we'd have, me being the go-getter, always on a mission, Michael at home toddling around, and I thought, 'I can't do this.'

Part of the reason I'd fallen for him was because he was such a regular guy, but my life was anything but regular and we argued like mad. He liked the quiet life, but he'd married a performer and I was out there in the public eye, being photographed, giving interviews, popping up all over the place. He hated it all.

Monet was only around eight months old when I decided to leave. I took her and went to my mum's house. I was a mess, broken, crying like a baby, devastated the dream was over. I loved Michael and wanted things to work, but I just couldn't see a future for us together, not if he didn't share my dream.

After a couple of months I moved back in, thinking we could try again, but nothing changed. I'm too driven to be with someone who isn't, so I left again, and this time I knew it was over. It was the worst feeling in the world, wanting things to work out with someone and finally having to accept they never would.

Get What You Want – and Keep it

A lot of the time the biggest challenge isn't about getting what you want, it's keeping it. Sometimes success can land in your lap – but sustaining it is hard. It's the same with anything in life, whether it's the job you've set your heart on or the relationship you're so desperate to have. You might get them but can you hang onto them? If that sounds familiar, you're not alone.

I've been through it with my career and with my relationships and I think every time something goes wrong and we lose the thing we were so desperate to have, it's life's way of teaching us something.

I remember seeing people in the music business having massive hits, being more successful than me, but they're all gone now. A lot of people get to where they want to be only to burn out and end up right back where they started. Hanging onto success is as much about grafting, putting in the work, as anything.

I've had a lot of disappointment in my relationships. So far, I haven't been able to get it right. I've attracted men who are weaker than me, men who liked the idea of a strong woman, and it's taken me a long time to appreciate that the best relationships are the ones where two strong, independent souls come together to make a whole. Where one person is counting on the other to somehow fix them or make up for what's missing in their life, it's never going to work. I'm living proof.

I've met a lot of men who've been impressed with my fame and I've given them a way into that flash, celebrity world. I'm not saying that's all it's ever been about, but it's been a factor all the same and I can see that now. Sometimes I've wondered if the man I've been with would have given me a second look if I'd been on the checkout at his local supermarket – if I'd still been Michelle Wallen – and, at times, I doubt it.

A lot of the time I've attracted star seekers, men who aren't secure in themselves, immature men who like the shiny, superficial stuff a bit too much. I hate all that, but I've still been taken in time after time.

I think all strong women have problems when it comes to finding a man who'll love them for what they are and not feel threatened by them.

The truth is, strong women tend to attract weak men.

Any time someone comes along and really batters you emotionally it's because they're weak. They see your strength and independence and they want it and, in the process, they end up breaking you in two. I've been in relationships with people looking to me to make them feel better about themselves, more self-important, using me as a means to get to where they want to be. And my weakness has been going along with it.

A lot of the time I've gone into relationships when I've been an emotional wreck, a complete mess. Part of it was to do with being young and immature. I was 21 when I rushed into marriage to try and fill the emotional void in my life and when that ended I went straight into another relationship, even though I was still broken and nowhere near ready to love again.

I'm older and wiser now and, looking back, the relationships I've had, even the bad ones, have given me something positive. There's been a huge amount of growth and learning going on at the same time as all the heartache. I can now see I've attracted men with massive insecurities, but I've also had insecurities of my own. I've tended to define myself through my career as well as whoever I'm with, which I think a lot of women do. Basically, my self-esteem has been bound up in my work so when my career's going well I feel good and when it's not I feel like crap. At those moments I've made some very poor choices, attracting people who are in just as bad a way as I am, even if they're doing a good job of covering it up.

You might wonder how I can keep falling for guys who are star seekers. The answer is they're very good at pretending they're really not bothered about the whole fame thing and I'm very good at believing them.

I've always tended to immerse myself too much in the man I'm with, always made it all about the guy, and put my own stuff on hold. I'm a giver, I like being generous and taking care of people, but what's happened is I've tended to *over* give.

In an ideal relationship, you're with someone who does as much for you as you do for them

In an ideal relationship, you're with someone who does as much for you as you do for them, but finding the balance can be hard. I've not managed it yet, getting to that place of being on equal terms, having the right amount of give and take on both sides.

One of us – usually me, although not always – has had more power.

I've been with men where it's turned into a power struggle. Suddenly, they're competing with you, jealous that you have the money, the status, the fame, or whatever it is. We still live in a sexist society and a lot of men don't like feeling they're being eclipsed by a woman. They have to be the dominant one in the relationship, the one holding the cards. When you're with the right person, someone who is confident and developed, you're not going to get that power struggle.

I still believe there are men out there who are successful, financially independent, secure in themselves, who aren't looking to define themselves through another person. They don't need to be with someone to feel powerful. They already *are* powerful. They have the self-assurance that comes from knowing their own worth. That's the kind of man who'll want to be with me for who I really am, not what's on the surface, and he's out there somewhere.

I'm so old-fashioned. I believe in loyalty and integrity and respect. I've got a strong moral code. I want to be a good person, do the right thing. I was brought up to be honest and truthful. My grandparents always said, 'Never tell a lie. If you tell one, you have to tell another and another and it never stops.' I believe in commitment and marriage. Doesn't matter how good-looking the guy is, if none of that counts for him, it's not going to work.

Love Takes Time

I don't believe there's such a thing as a quick-fix for anything in life. I know from experience it doesn't work. All you're doing is finding a short-term solution to whatever the problem is and it's not going to last. Diets are a quick-fix. Relationships can be, too.

We're all looking for instant gratification, but we have to get over that because it's not the way to long-term fulfilment. Sometimes when we're in a bad place we settle for anything, and end up with people who aren't right for us just because we think it's better than being alone.

Sometimes, though, being alone is the best thing for us because that's when we get to know who we really are. I'm finally having such a beautiful relationship with myself and I'm now aware that's the one I have to get right first. It takes time to accept yourself, to get to see the things you like – and the things you really don't.

> Get a **good** **relationship** with **yourself** and you have a much **better chance** of **finding** the right person

Get a good relationship with yourself and you have a much better chance of finding the right person to share your life. The best relationships are when the woman has her thing going on and the man has his. It's not about control or manipulating one another. It's about each one fulfilling their potential and respecting one another. Neither one feels threatened by the other's success because they have their own sense of security, independence, and self-worth. Two people like that won't suck the life out of each other.

I'm looking for a relationship where I don't lose myself. I think once you become mature you start to want different things from a partner anyway. When you're young it's all about sex, but as you get older and your priorities change sex becomes just one aspect of being with someone. I actually think what's more important is engaging on lots of levels, feeling a connection with the heart, the mind, and the spirit. It's about feeling you've found a partner in crime, that you're both on a wonderful journey together, that you've got a real *partnership*.

The relationships that work are about two people working at life together, going in the same direction, sharing the same dreams. Being in sync with another person is such a sexy thing and if you find that in your life then you really are blessed.

It's about spending time with someone, getting to know them – not just the bits you can see on the surface – going through stuff together, good and bad, surviving the hard times. When you've been through shit and you still want to be with that person, *that's* love. Real love takes time.

Real love grows and develops.

Some people don't seem to get that today. They think if they're not feeling it straight away it's not right, but you don't feel love at once. How can you detect something so deep instantly? I honestly believe you should never be impressed with the thing that happens fastest – and that goes for love too.

When you're in a loving partnership it's about trust, loyalty, commitment, integrity, friendship; these things take time. If it all happens too quickly and you get that crazy *ohmygod* feeling, it's the first sign it's wrong.

Part of the problem right now is we're too quick to jump into love and too quick to jump out when things get rocky. Not every relationship is going to last, but when you've got something that's worth having it doesn't make sense to throw in the towel at the first sign of trouble.

I've been in a relationship where my partner had an affair and we worked through things. I'm not saying affairs are right; they're not. But they don't have to be the end either.

We're in such a disposable society that we're used to getting rid of things even before they're broken. We want the next model, the shiny new one with more features. Half the time we don't want to make an effort to sort out what's going wrong with the stuff – relationships included – we already have.

I don't actually think affairs solve anything. They usually result from having a problem you can't deal with, they're a way to take away the pain and feel better. It's an easy way out in the short-term. Affairs happen when someone is weak, afraid of intimacy, and looking for something where there's no commitment. They're a means of escape.

Not everyone can get over an affair, I know, but to me it's not the end of the world. What matters more is if you still love each other and want a life together. All relationships are going to have their moments when things go wrong, but if they have a solid foundation of love you can get beyond the bad stuff.

I grew up with my grandparents and if I could create a relationship like the one they had I'd be happy. My grandad is dead now, but he and my grandmother were together for more than 50 years and they absolutely adored each other. They had their times when they'd fall out, but they were in it for the long-haul and I watched them fall in love all over again in their twilight years. She'd walk into a room and my grandad, this tough, bible-bashing dude, would just melt. He was *butter* when she was around. They loved each other to bits. That's what I call real love.

It's Not Working

When one relationship after another goes wrong, what's that telling you? It doesn't mean all men are rubbish, but that you're attracting the wrong ones and you need to work out why. Don't just blame the other person – take responsibility.

The more conscious you become and the more you work on yourself, the more chance you'll have of getting it right next time. Maybe you need some time on your own to get to know who you are and what you want.

I've had a habit of jumping from one relationship to another without giving myself the space to work out what went wrong, then finding I've got problems all over again. I didn't even know I was doing it. I just wanted love, but I was looking in all the wrong places. How many of us have done the same thing?

When your heart breaks it's the worst feeling in the world. You're broken, lying there in pieces. You think you'll never get over it. You feel like the most worthless, ugly, person in the world.

- *Don't* give in to those feelings because if you do they'll destroy you.
- *Trust* that however bad you feel it's only temporary.
- *Think* yourself better.
- *Never* lose sight of your goal.
- *Keep* doing the work.

When You're Down

When things crash it's easy to let yourself get dragged under, keep replaying the bad stuff in your head, sitting there thinking, he/she/they did me wrong, feeling the pain, hurting all over again. Yes, they did you wrong but you have to move on. You can't let depression take hold.

A few years ago I used to think you just had to wait for depression to move, but I don't anymore. I really believe you have to fight it, kick it out. Depression is wallowing, it's a pity party, and it doesn't serve you in any way. If you let it in, it *will* dominate you and take you over. I know people who get so down they close the curtains and stay in bed.

You can't do that. Get up and fight it. Push yourself, even if it feels like it's going to kill you. Open the curtains, let in some light, and get out of the house. Do something, go for a walk, help someone, just keep moving. If you leave those curtains shut, before you know it you will have been in bed for a week, then a month, then six months. Then a year goes by and you haven't been out and, believe me, you're not going to feel any better.

When I get depressed, it's the end. That's how I feel, but I don't wallow in it. I get up and do something. What works for me is replacing the awful feelings with something better. I go to the gym, go for a walk, get on the computer and do some research, read a book, whatever. I just don't stay in the funk because I know that when I move it's going to start to shift.

I was given Prozac after my breakdown, but I really didn't like it. It made me feel numb and disconnected. I was hallucinating, hearing voices, and it frightened me so much I stopped taking it. There has to be another way. I met someone who told me he'd been on anti-depressants for 20 years and that he was absolutely fine. All I can say is he didn't look fine to me.

When depression comes it feeds itself and everything starts playing on your mind, going round and round in your head, all the things from the past that went wrong. Suddenly, it's not just the relationship that's broken up that's bothering you, it's the teacher who said you were no good when you were 10 years old, or the boss who wouldn't promote you. It's everything.

I'm not saying it's easy because I've been there, more than once, and it's a horrible, horrible thing, but you have to stop internalising stuff because it doesn't help you. It makes you feel more depressed and, if you let it, depression will kill you. I've seen it first-hand.

I had a cousin, a few years older than me, who was my best buddy. We used to hang out together, go to parties; he was the sweetest guy. A few months after I'd signed my record deal I was in a car going to the studio to work on my first single, *My One Temptation*, and as I was going past Earl's Court station I saw him. I knew he'd been through a bad time, that he'd walked in on his wife in bed with his best friend. She was the love of his life, and he was heartbroken.

I jumped out of the car and ran over and, I don't know why but he just didn't look right to me. His trousers were a bit short, his shirt didn't fit, his shoes were wrong. All his clothes looked too small for him. We chatted, and even though he was pretending he was okay I knew he wasn't so I gave him some cigarettes, then I took off as I had to go and work in the studio. I didn't know that would be the last time I would see him.

He got on a train and headed miles out of London, walked along a motorway, and ended up in some woods where he spent the night. He died from hypothermia. He was 27 years old. It was the first time I'd lost someone I loved.

Accept you'll have your bad days – we all do – and when they come, fight back. You can't allow other people to poison you, ruin your life, make you ill. I had an aunty who'd been with her partner for 20 years, always wanted a baby with him, but it hadn't happened. Then he went and had an affair, the girl had a baby, and it broke my aunty's heart. The next thing she was in hospital for a heart bypass, and she died. She was only 45. That's why you have to stand up to heartache and depression. You *can* take the power back.

It's easy to think that where you are right now is all that exists, but you never know what's round the corner. A friend of mine who was flat broke killed herself because she couldn't see a way through her financial problems. The next day money she wasn't expecting came through. You have to trust that things will get better because *they always do*. I've had 20 years in the music industry and I've lost count of the number of times I've been told I was finished, a has-been, all washed-up. I've lost two record deals, been flat broke, gone bankrupt, had my heartbroken, and I'm still here. *Never* write yourself off.

It doesn't matter how bad things get, I never lose my sense of self-belief. We all have that in us, some more than others, but you have to find it and hold onto it. I can be on the floor, crying, wanting to kill myself, and there's still something deep down telling me I'll get over it, that everything's going to work out.

What you have to remember is that the dark times are a sign of something good on the way. You just have to hang on and let it pass. It's like giving birth. You go into labour, the pains are killing you and you don't want to have the baby anymore, you just want the pain to stop. Then you give birth, you've got your baby, and you're not thinking about the labour pains any more. They're forgotten.

That's exactly how life is.

We Are What We Think

Thoughts are incredibly powerful. The way we think creates our reality, so if you spend your time wallowing and believing things will never get better, you're making things much harder for yourself than they need be.

Don't dwell on the reasons you have to feel *bad*. Think about the stuff that makes you feel *good*. Put a support system in place so that when you're in a funk there's someone you can call who'll help pull you out of it. I have my sisters and my mother and I know that just talking to them is going to make me feel better.

Try not to make everything about you. Focus your attention on other people. Is there somebody who needs your help? Helping another person is guaranteed to take your mind off your stuff and, when you stop *thinking* about what's bothering you, you start *feeling* better.

We're all really good at feeding ourselves negative stuff. Something goes wrong and that's all we can think about. How many times have you given yourself a hard time because you think you're not good enough? Too many, probably. And how often do you say anything nice to yourself? Probably never.

Sometimes you have to stop and take stock, just look at the great things you've done and be thankful. We forget how much we've achieved in life when we're in a bad place. You have to remind yourself and reflect only on the good; that's what builds your self-esteem.

Why would you want to dwell on bad stuff? All that's going to do is make you feel worse. A friend was telling me he was feeling low, not feeling like he'd achieved much. I said, 'When was the last time you checked all the things you've done?'

He looked at me and said, 'I never do that.'

'That's the problem right there. Tonight, when you get home, take out the albums and the photographs, take the awards out of the cupboard and look at them. Look at the videos. Remind yourself.'

We all have to do that, just get off the treadmill that's life and stop for a minute.

If I'm feeling a bit moody, I'll look through my albums, put a video on, maybe listen to my Radio 2 show, and it makes me appreciate the good things I've done.

How often do you look back at photographs that bring back great memories? Hardly ever? Never? Get out the album and look at the pictures from 10 years ago when you were on some farm in Scotland or in the Himalayas or wherever it was. Bring back the good memories. We all have them. It may be a holiday, your wedding day, your baby's christening. Get the pictures out and replay it. We all have things we're good at. Are you a good mother? A good wife? A good sister? A good friend? A good daughter? Take time to think about what you do well, whatever it might be.

Focus on Your Goals

Remind yourself what it is you want to do with your life and don't let anything distract you. If you're serious about success, you have to be focused. There's always going to be stuff that comes along and knocks you off course. Setbacks and pitfalls are there to test you, that's all; they're not the end of the world. Just don't fall into the trap of thinking it's all hopeless and you might as well give up. Don't be a victim.

I've been friends with the sprinter Linford Christie for years and I remember him saying that when he's on the track before a race he doesn't see the people either side of him or the spectators. All he sees is the lane in front of him and the tape at the end of it. That's how we all have to think.

Focus on where you want to go and don't let anything get in the way.

Men have been my distraction in the past and I've been putting my own stuff on hold while I take care of them. When we do that we're never even going to get to the end of the race, never mind win it.

So, work out what your goal is and keep taking steps towards making it happen. Don't just think about what you want to achieve – write it down. Keep a journal and get into the habit of reading it every two or three days. When you have an idea, put it in the journal and keep going back to it. Writing down your goals and dreams is incredibly powerful. It may seem like a small thing, but seeing things on paper makes them feel real.

All of us have that thing where we want what we can't have or what's not good for us. I've been there so many times in my relationships, falling for the wrong guys, trying to make things work, loving too hard, making it all about them – and ending up in a heap on the floor.

I didn't know what I was doing wrong, but now I know I was focusing on the wrong things. I was falling in love with people for their talent and not looking hard enough at what kind of a character they were. Some of the men I've been involved with have been shallow and superficial, but that's not what I saw.

What I saw was a great musician or a director, or whatever they happened to be. I used to think if somebody was talented they were also good, that having a gift came with a sensibility of being loving and kind. I saw my own gift – my voice – as God-given, and I was humble about it. I thought it was the same for everyone. Big mistake.

Talent is just talent; you don't have to be nice with it. I can see that now, but I couldn't for a long time. Now I know that the essence of a person is more important than their talent. I still love talented people. Seeing somebody who's genius at what they do is very seductive, but I'm learning to look beyond that, go a bit deeper and I think I can spot the ones who have got the talent but not much else. They're the ones with butter on their lips.

I'm also aware, though, that attraction knocks you sideways and gets in the way of rational thinking. So many times you end up thinking, why did I fall for him when he was just going to hurt me? It's usually because that person came along to give you that wake-up call and, if you're paying attention, you're going to learn something, even if it's a painful lesson.

Sometimes you have to go through it because what comes afterwards is amazing.

So, sometimes when the worst thing happens – the guy leaves, you lose your job, you end up broke – it's exactly what you needed to help you take another step on the road to where you want to be.

What I've Learned

- The best relationships are about two people working at life together, going in the same direction, sharing the same dreams

- Never lose sight of your goal

- Money means nothing without love

- Real love takes time

Loving & Learning

I was a really unhappy child.

I remember feeling sad all the time. I grew up with my grandparents and I loved them, and had a good life with them, but I was the youngest of three sisters and I had this thing about feeling inferior, like I was invisible.

I felt unloved and I was always crying. I'd sit on the stairs and cry for hours. I was a really sickly kid as well. I had eczema all over my body and sometimes I'd move and my skin would crack and bleed. I was bandaged up all the time and underneath the dressings was this awful reptilian skin. I had so many things wrong with me and was constantly at the hospital. I had nasal problems, trouble breathing, all the stuff with my skin, and allergies. If I walked into someone's house and they'd just put the vacuum cleaner round I'd be wheezing and gasping. I never felt well and I cried over anything. If my grandmother went to the shops, it would be enough to have me in floods of tears.

I always felt sorry for myself, always felt sad, absolutely wallowed in misery. I had this real victim mentality and all it did was make me feel worse. I know now it doesn't pay to be like that.

I really suffered with eczema until one day my grandad prayed really hard for me and my grandmother took me to the beach in Brighton and bathed me in the sea. My skin cleared up just like that. The only time it flared up after that was when I was just about to release my first single, *My One Temptation*, in 1988, and I had a tiny bit on my hands but it didn't last long. I was so nervous, so scared the record wouldn't do well, and I think that's what triggered it.

I really believe our emotional state has everything to do with our health. When I was a child it was my mum and dad I really wanted to live with, but they weren't together. They'd visit, bring loads of presents, spoil us rotten – and go again. I hated that bit, when they went and I'd sit there in tears thinking, I don't care about the presents, it's you I want.

When my parents were younger they were amazing, really glamorous. My dad was like a young Quincy Jones and my mum looked like Diana Ross. There was this whole scene going on among the black community of south London back then and my parents were right in the thick of it. Everyone dressed really well, went to certain clubs, and lived their lives in the fast lane. It was showbiz on a street level.

I grew up in awe of my dad. I really thought he was Superman. He'd come to pick us up and he always had a different car. One week it was a Cadillac, the next an E-Type Jag or an Aston Martin. When you're a kid and the whole street is out watching your dad in his flash car, it's pretty amazing. I was obsessed with him. I loved the way he had this distinctive smell of cigars mixed with aftershave. Even when I was little, I knew he had impeccable taste. Oh man, his clothes: silk trousers, crocodile shoes, always the best of everything. He was so good-looking, so exotic, like something out of the movies.

When he visited it was like Christmas because he always had presents and they were never anything normal, like a cuddly toy. He went to America quite a lot and he'd bring back expensive hi-fi systems, stuff you didn't get here. He was always so impressive.

We'd get in the car and he'd take us to Mayfair, which was like another world. We'd go to Hyde Park and look at the pavement art. Sometimes we'd go on a boat trip. I was so in love with my dad. I knew he was special, that he was cultured and talented. He painted, he wrote, he sang, he was a musician.

At home with my grandparents I listened to gospel music. With my dad I listened to everything, from the Isley Brothers to Tchaikovsky. I remember him putting on Dizzy Gillespie or Miles Davis records and playing along on the flute or trumpet.

My grandparents lived in a lovely Victorian house, but it was my dad's mews house that struck me as cool. With my grandparents it was Jamaican food – rice and peas and chicken. With my dad it was smoked salmon, truffles, and sauces made from mushrooms and wine. I'd never tasted anything like it. He opened my eyes to a different world.

He was around a lot of the time, but it wasn't enough for me and I was paranoid that my sister was his favourite. Sometimes he'd take her out and leave me behind and I'd sit there crying.

I hated seeing him go. When he went through the door there were always tears. I loved him but at the same time I felt rejected and abandoned, and that made it a complicated relationship.

I still struggle with abandonment. It's a big one for me. I don't want to be left so I'm always the one to end relationships. Fear makes me leave first.

Where Were You?

I started feeling like I didn't really like my parents anymore when I was around 14. I used to see a lot of my mum, spend weekends with her, and her house was a real party centre. She always had lots of people round having fun, but suddenly I didn't want it anymore. I didn't understand why she hadn't been around as much as I wanted her to be when I was younger, and I got angry about it. I'd look at her and say, 'Where were you?' I didn't understand that she was just doing the best she could the only way she knew how.

Things changed between me and my dad when I started seeing who he really was, when I realised he wasn't straight, that he was a bad man, I was devastated.

I'm very straightforward and conventional. I do everything by the book. I was brought up by my grandparents to live a clean life and I hate the idea of breaking the law. Here was someone with a brilliant mind, talented in loads of different ways, and he wasn't using any of it. I was so disappointed in him. When I got my record deal my dad was around a lot and I'd get him to help me out, give him a cheque to pay someone, and he'd disappear with it. This went on for years, me giving him money, bailing him out when he was in trouble, then not seeing him for ages. He always had some story about why he needed money and, every time, I'd be taken in. He was conning me, but he was charming and charismatic with it. He was my dad and I loved him.

I was making a lot of money and I thought I could use it to make the family get along, bring everyone together. I had this massive house and everyone would come round and hang out – very much like my mum's place used to be – and it was nice until people started ripping me off. In the end I thought, 'Hang on, do you want a family so bad you're willing to let yourself be walked over?' That's when I started putting my foot down.

The final straw with my dad came when I lost my deal with EMI and I was broke, on my face, wondering how I was going to make ends meet. One day he borrowed my car, which was the only asset I had, and didn't bring it back. That was *it*. Never again.

My relationship with my dad is the most painful and difficult one I've ever experienced. After everything I went through you'd think he'd be the kind of man I'd steer well clear of, but all my life the guys I've gone for have been just like him.

Andreas

Andreas was so like my dad. Good-looking, charming, cultured; he even had the same familiar scent of cigars and aftershave. I was an emotional wreck when I met him – broke, no work, on my own with a child. I wasn't sure of him to start with. I thought he was a player, too flashy, too clever and manipulative. There was something a bit distant about him. I'd experienced it all before, with my dad and almost every other relationship I'd had, and that made me wary, but Andreas wouldn't take no for an answer. He wanted us to be together and he chased and chased until we were. Somewhere, a long way off, I could hear warning bells ringing, but I decided not to listen to them.

I'd always been the breadwinner in the past, involved with men who hadn't got their careers going and couldn't pay the bills, and for the first time in my life I'd met a man who wanted to take care of me and provide for me and my daughter.

Andreas came along when I had nothing and no idea what I was going to do, and he took care of me. He was the first man to make me feel I didn't have to worry about money and that really touched me. I thought it could work between us, even though we weren't going into things on an even footing. He had the power and the money and I had nothing.

We met in 1999 and had seven years together. I thought we'd be together forever. I had some of my best times with him, and some of my worst, but I learned so much from that relationship. The big ones, the ones that break you in two, always teach you the most.

I wanted to help Andreas and did what I've done so many times before – made it all about him. That's where my energy and focus was. I took him round, opened doors, and introduced him to people. My friends became his. I sang at the launch of his company. He was a gifted photographer and we'd pour over his pictures together, honing his talent, studying the work of people like Annie Liebowitz, and he got better and better until he became an absolute genius.

He was there for me, too, encouraging me, pushing me, putting me first. When we met I was depressed, devastated about losing my record deal, and gutted that *Black Angel* wasn't the hit I wanted it to be. Five years of my life had gone into making it, it was the first thing I'd produced myself, and when it didn't take off it was like losing a child.

I didn't want to sing anymore. Being a mum, shopping, cooking, cleaning, looking after Andreas, was more appealing. I thought I'd had it with making records. He changed my mind.

He didn't just encourage me to sing again, he made it happen, bought out my management deal, took over my career, and put up the money to make an album. No one had ever done so much for me and I was deeply moved.

We went to New York to work on the album, but something just wasn't right. Music had always been such a massive thing for me but with *If I Could Love You* I just wasn't feeling it. It was like I wasn't firing on all cylinders, but even though, inside, I didn't feel good I went along with it because it was what Andreas wanted.

I don't actually like the album, but I don't regret making it. Sometimes, for all kinds of reasons, the work you produce doesn't turn out the way you want it to, but that doesn't mean you shouldn't have gone there in the first place.

The whole thing about creating, whatever it is you're doing, is that there's no certainty, no guaranteed outcome. You don't have to stop, though. You just have to understand when you're having a lean time, that the lows aren't going to be forever, and that when the highs come and you get it right again, you're going to appreciate it even more.

Good Times, Bad Times

It's never easy to put your finger on the exact moment when things start to go wrong between two people, but I think with Andreas we were setting up problems from the start because we weren't on an equal footing. I now know that co-dependent relationships don't work.

I've tried them plenty of times in the past where I've been the provider and the guy I'm with has been dependent and, what might seem fine at first, is never going to work long-term. When one person holds all the cards, it always makes the other frustrated and resentful and the very strength of character they admired in you to begin with only serves to make them feel weak.

With Andreas, I was the weak one and he was in control. I was grateful that he was taking care of me, paying the bills, giving me his credit card to go shopping. It probably sounds like the perfect arrangement, and I'm sure it works for some people but you need balance in relationships because without it you're in trouble.

I felt bad that it wasn't *my* credit card, that I had *no* money of my own, that I was *dependent* on him for everything. I was living in a big house in Notting Hill Gate, Andreas paying for everything, looking after me and Monet, but I wasn't happy. I felt like I was under his thumb and the money side of things bothered me. On paper, we were the perfect couple, but the reality was it didn't work.

Believe me, you might think it all sounds wonderful, but that level of dependency doesn't bring happiness. I wasn't fulfilling my potential. I had all these things I wanted to do and I felt stuck. I could see things going well for Andreas, but I couldn't seem to make anything happen for myself.

Feeling powerless did nothing for my self-worth and that made me lash out. When we argued I was always raising the stakes, threatening to leave, because walking away was the only power I still had.

Affairs of the Heart

When you're young it's the flashy stuff that catches your eye, but once you get a bit more mature it starts to lose its lustre – and that goes for men, too. I've always been attracted to men like my dad, but as I get older I'm after someone who's more solid and down to earth, like my grandad.

Andreas was a mixture of the two.

Like my dad, he loved the good things in life, had a taste for adventure, and took me on some amazing trips all over the world. He was smart, too, well-read, able to engage my mind in the same way my dad does and, like my dad, he had a flip side that was total chaos.

Like my grandad he took care of finances and made sure we never lacked for anything. I thought my prince had come and was completely besotted.

We had five good years before we started to have serious problems, but I always believed we could get through anything. In the beginning we were on a journey together, but as time wore on we were going in different directions. He's a free spirit and I respected that. I think one of the reasons we were together for so long was because I'm not the kind of woman to chase a man down. I think a man either wants to be with me or he doesn't.

Andreas was working away a lot and I didn't enjoy the separations – they reminded me of my dad not being around – but I never stood in his way. Why would I? My friends thought I was too trusting, giving him all that freedom, but I can't be checking up on someone all the time, phoning, wanting to know where they are and who they're with. That's not my idea of a relationship. It's not my idea of love.

> Just because a **person** has **faults,** doesn't mean they can't be loved

I think sometimes if you give a man a shiny new toy they stop playing with the old one, like in the film *Toy Story*. That's what Andreas was like; he'd see something new, think he could have some fun and still come back to me. When I found out that he'd been seeing someone else and it came to the crunch, it was our relationship he wanted to save. We both did.

We all have weaknesses, some more than others. It may be alcohol or drugs or sex or gambling or any number of things. I'm not condoning any of it but what I am saying is, just because a person has faults, doesn't mean they can't be loved. It doesn't mean they don't have a good heart and plenty of other good qualities. It doesn't mean they don't love you.

An affair creates real cracks in a relationship. I know that first-hand. Getting things back on track, even if you still love each other and want to be together, can be the hardest thing.

I'm not trying to tell anyone else what to do because we're all different and only you know what's right for you. But, at that point in my life, I was with him for the long haul and didn't want to give up. I just didn't feel we were at the end of the line.

It was never about persuading him to stay because I don't believe in that. It was about what we both wanted.

The Past Repeats Itself

A lot of the stuff I'd been through in my other relationships came up with Andreas. Over the years I've met movie stars, artists, all kinds of celebrities, rubbed shoulders, hung out with them. Some of them are great, some aren't, but, basically, they're just the same as the rest of us. That's something my dad always taught me.

What I call 'the lights' don't dazzle me. I love to rave as much as anyone, but I got tired of endless partying a long time ago. Most of the time I'm happy at home just chilling out. I enjoy the simple stuff in life: cooking, sitting down to dinner with the people I love. I like eating out now and then, but I don't need to do it every night. When I met Andreas he was eating out all the time. He wanted to party all the time, too. I've learned from experience that the entertainment industry and everything to do with it – music, television, fashion, media – is full of people out for themselves. It's a world where nobody cares about anyone else.

How many times have you tried to change someone? It doesn't work. It doesn't matter what you're living with – alcoholism, drug abuse, gambling, infidelity, whatever it might be – you can't fix it. All you can do is turn your own stuff around and fix yourself.

Is it Me?

We have to accept people for what they are. Putting our own lives on hold, waiting for someone else to change, is a waste of time.

For a long time I thought I was to blame for the problems in our relationship. I kept thinking, 'Is it me?' And sometimes it was, but it's never just one person's fault when things go wrong.

We all have to take responsibility for our lives. Andreas did a lot of stuff I didn't like, but blaming him for everything doesn't help either of us. Too often, we don't take responsibility for our actions.

Things go wrong and we spend our time going, 'Oh, he did me wrong.' Well, maybe he did, but it's never one-sided, and it takes a strong person to own up and say, 'Okay, I think some of this mess is mine.'

A lot of the problems I had with Andreas stemmed from me going into the relationship financially screwed. I'm so independent I just didn't enjoy that role. My ego couldn't handle the fact that he had all the money. I'd always been the provider, the independent chick, taking care of everybody else, and I was angry I was broke. I didn't like it.

Being powerless battered my self-worth. I felt unattractive. I comfort ate and put on weight. I didn't look good. I felt as if the life was being sucked out of me and because of that there were times when I really wasn't kind to Andreas, pushing him away, threatening to leave.

I was resentful, but I think he was, too. When you live, eat, drink and sleep another person it's not healthy. No wonder he went outside. He wanted some air. I was stifled, too. I had so many dreams, but nothing was moving. I kept asking God what was going on and now I can see that what was blocking me was being with Andreas. That's not to blame him – it's just that he and I *together* were the problem.

He had issues with commitment, but it's only now I've realised that's a problem for me, too. I'm very loyal, very conventional, but my fear of being abandoned means I struggle with commitment. I like to have control, feel I can hold my own within a relationship, and if I don't, well, it doesn't work for me. Basically, if I don't hold the cards – and I held none of the cards with Andreas – I'm not going to commit.

Same Old, Same Old

What you experience as a child shapes the relationships you have later on, but it can take a while to work it out. Think about the relationship *you* had with *your* father. Was he around? Did you feel loved and secure or rejected and abandoned? How did your parents get along? Were they together?

Were they happy? Was your dad good to your mum? My parents split up when I was small and my dad battered my mum emotionally. I hated not having them around, seeing them come in and out of my life.

Don't feel bad if you seem to be making the same mistake time and again, falling for the same kind of man, ending up in pain. What that's telling you is you're still learning and every time it happens you're finding out a bit more about yourself. You end up stopping and thinking, 'Okay, he did some atrocious things and broke me in two and it was awful, but *I* invited him into my life and *I* allowed him to do those things, so what's the message?'

You might only get some of the answers and have to go through it all again before you start to see what's really going on. When you keep repeating the same stuff it just means you still have work to do on yourself, that you haven't yet found the answers you need to be able to move on.

It's a tough one but, whatever happens, you can't get bitter. Bitterness is dark and destructive. It's wrong and the only one it hurts is *you*. It's another sign of letting your emotions control you. You have to put a lid on them or you get stuck in the pain, and the longer you stay there the harder it is to move on. It's the emotional equivalent of staying in bed with the curtains shut. You end up in a dark place, not getting on with your life, not fulfilling your purpose, just wallowing.

In those dark moments when you hate the guy who hurt you and you feel like hurting him back, cutting up his clothes, doing something crazy, try to remind yourself that you used to love him. That's why you were together, remember? Hating him, blaming him, is a waste of energy. You probably know exactly what his issues are, but don't focus on what's wrong with him. They're *his* problems, not *yours*, and he'll sort them out if he wants to.

Focus on your own issues instead. When you love someone you have to let him sort his own things out. He's on his own journey and if he's messing up, that's up to him. It doesn't mean you stop caring, it just means accepting that you can't do anything about it, even if you can see he's hurting himself on the way. We don't own anyone and we have to know when to let go.

I got so much growth from being with Andreas. I know now that I'm not always the easiest person to live with, that I can be dominant and pushy, a bit of a bully sometimes, and I don't mind admitting it. No one's perfect, but at least once we become aware of our faults we can try to do something about them.

Just because you love someone, doesn't mean you can have a life with them. If it starts to feel like they're dragging you down, your survival instinct has to kick in. You can't stay with someone who keeps hurting you, however much you care for them.

There are men around who are secure in themselves. They know their worth and don't need to define themselves through the woman they're with. They're mature and powerful in their own right. They've got to where they are in life through their own efforts, not by riding on someone else's back, and they're not about to start now. They're real alpha males, not gamma males pretending, and they're not threatened by an alpha female. I don't say they're easy to find, but they're definitely out there and when I meet the right one I'll know because it'll be me he falls in love with, not the lights.

Men and Mid-Life Crisis

I think, generally, men have a harder time getting old than women, and that especially goes for the cute ones, the ones used to getting a lot of attention. Their sense of self, their status and success is so tied up in how they look that when they see age creeping up they panic. That's why you get guys coming up to 40 who suddenly go a bit crazy.

They're not the centre of attention anymore and it freaks them out. They see younger guys coming along, stealing the limelight, and they can't take it, so they look for ways of making themselves feel better. It comes down to basic insecurity and low self-worth, a deep-rooted fear that all they really have going for them is on the surface.

They measure themselves in terms of vanity and what they *have*, not what they *are*. When they start losing their hair, getting a few lines, seeing the younger guys overtaking them, the ego doesn't like it and the ego is really powerful. It's never satisfied. How many times have you seen a guy splash out on a really ostentatious car when he hits middle age? Or go off with a younger woman? They think it's the answer, that the external stuff is going to fill the void, make them feel better, but it can't. Then, when the car or the new girl doesn't do the trick, they have to look for something else and so it goes on.

Actually, all they have to do is to come to terms with the idea of age, accept it as a natural process that doesn't have to hold you back. Getting old is about wisdom and experience and that's how the guys I was talking about earlier, the ones that really know their worth, see it.

They put more value on what's going on inside and they have the confidence to know the world isn't judging them purely on physical appearance. Some of the most charismatic and sexy men don't have classic good looks. Their attraction is deep-rooted.

It's tough when the guy you love goes off the rails, starts acting like a stranger, swaps the family saloon for a sports car, leaves you for someone younger. Of course you're going to wonder what's going on. You're going to think, 'Is it me? Am I too old/too ugly/not good enough?'

His insecurities and paranoia are going to make you feel bad, at least in the short-term until you work out what's going on. It's painful, but you can't allow his low self-worth to rob you of yours. You have to go home to yourself and work out what's really going on. The chances are it's not even about you – it's about him. What's going on is his struggle to come to terms with the negative feelings he has about himself.

A mid-life crisis is a bit like a breakdown in some ways. It's not about thinking straight or being rational, taking stock of your life, realising that the good stuff actually outweighs the bad. The bad starts to dominate and take hold. It's like having a garden choked with weeds. There might be some beautiful plants in there, but you can't see them anymore. That's why a guy will abandon the long-standing relationship, turn his back on a stable, loving home, and swap security for something a bit more on the edge. It makes him feel he's still out there, a player, that he's still got what it takes.

I'm not even sure those guys know what they're doing. I don't think they set out to hurt anyone. They're not thinking about the carnage they've left behind. They're just lost, trying to make themselves feel better, and hoping the car, the girl, or whatever it is, is going to do the trick.

Be Forgiving

When people hurt us we have to learn to forgive. It's important to forgive because you let yourself off the hook at the same time. If I don't forgive it means I'm still angry inside, and I can't afford to have that energy in me. It won't help me.

Pain is part of life. We all have to experience it in order to learn and grow. None of us can avoid it, no matter how hard we try. When pain comes along, accept it. Walk through it. Keep going and you'll come out of that dark tunnel and into the light. We all have those moments, but it's always when you're at your lowest point, when things can't get any worse, that you start to turn the corner and life gives you something good.

Every time I get kicked or have some trauma and I'm in the darkest, most scary place, something amazing comes along. Life *is* scary. You never know what's coming, but the key is to keep going anyway, go round that blind bend in the road and deal with whatever is there. That's what it means to be alive. The way you get through the tough bits is by having faith, trusting you're on a journey with all its twists and turns, and holding onto your self-belief.

I still love my dad and spend hours talking to him about all kinds of stuff. We think the same, like the same books, love talking about philosophy, analysing human behaviour. In terms of how we think, we're very alike. Even when I was a child I remember having deep conversations with him and being fascinated by his ideas and observations. He's still the same.

Yes, I was angry and devastated each time he let me down, but it's in the past. It wouldn't serve me to hold onto those emotions. I'm better served by being compassionate, showing love and tolerance, and accepting that some people are less awake than others and more likely to cause pain. I actually thank my dad because what I went through with him has helped make me who I am now. We all need that stuff.

Letting Go

I've met women still angry with their parents, still blaming what went on in the past for the stuff going wrong in their lives now. They replay the bad times over and over, and end up hurt all over again by something that happened years ago. When you do that the wounds you have are never going to get a chance to heal. Letting go is one of the biggest lessons we can learn. You have to get to the point where you stop making your parents responsible for your stuff because they didn't get it right. Accept that no one got it right with them. Forgive them for not doing all the things you think they should have. Usually, they did the best they can and, maybe they did mess up, but don't we all sometimes? We don't know what our parents went through, but the chances are they also had their problems.

I was so angry with my mum when I was younger, lashing out – 'You don't love me, you're never here.' But now I know she also had it tough as a child. She's around more now than she ever was when I was a kid and the time we have together more than makes up for the past. We've done a lot of healing and we've got a great relationship now.

There's no point being angry forever. You're just hurting yourself. If you let go of the hurt, you might just end up with the relationship you missed out on when you were growing up.

My dad let me down, conned me so many times, and it was only when my life fell apart I decided I'd never let him do it again, but, whatever he did in the past, I can't stay angry with him. It's not going to make me feel better.

I know he's selfish and irresponsible and an opportunist and I also know he can't help himself. But that doesn't mean I can't help *myself* and make sure he never rips me off again.

He still frustrates me because he could have chosen to do great things with his life and he didn't. Part of that might have been because his mum died when he was in his teens; it's something he talks about all the time. Partly it's because he's just not good at seeing things through. He prefers the short cut.

My dad reminds me of how I used to be when I was little, when I'd cry all the time, and wallow, and be a victim. He thinks he didn't have the opportunities to make something great of his life, but I don't buy that. *That's* being a victim.

I know things aren't easy for black males in our society, but you just have to look around to see that plenty have still taken the right path and done well: the journalist and politician, Trevor Phillips; the designer, Ozwald Boateng; the writer and film-maker, Darkus Howe. There's no excuse, not for my dad, not for anyone.

Don't Be Afraid to Try

We can always make excuses for ourselves, but life is for living. It's about fulfilling your potential, having a go, even when things don't look good.

You can't let fear stop you from pursuing your dream. We're all going to trip up at some point, feel we're not getting anywhere, that everything's hopeless, but you can't be thrown off course.

I've failed loads of times, but it doesn't stop me. I've had four albums that didn't even make the Billboard 100, but at least I tried. It hurts me more when the music isn't the way I want it to be. I'm more disappointed that I didn't make a couple of albums the way I wanted to than I am about how many copies they sold.

When someone tells me they heard my record and they loved it and it touched them, *that* means more to me than any chart, and that's how you have to learn to look at things.

Never think you're average. There are a lot of people stuck in a mediocre mindset, afraid to push themselves. Sometimes all that's stopping you pass that exam with distinction is thinking you're only capable of scraping through. Never be afraid to have a go. If you don't succeed you can always try again – and again, and again.

I believe we're all capable of so much more than we're actually doing and so many times we're the ones holding ourselves back. If you have a great idea, pursue it. Just having it in the first place tells you that somewhere, deep down, you know you can do it.

So many people limit themselves. Fear holds them back. You have to get past that. If that's the way you're thinking, you're going to fail because *your thoughts are the most powerful thing in the universe*. Once you let negative thoughts in and start to believe them, you're setting yourself up to fail. Belief in yourself, faith in what you can do, tips the odds of success in your favour straight away.

You have to get tough on negativity, and not just your own, because negative thinking is a poison that spreads like wildfire. Every negative thing someone says to you takes root if you dwell on it. You tell someone your idea, they ridicule it, and suddenly you've lost faith. Don't let the cynics put you off. Make sure you have positive people in your life who'll embrace whatever it is you're trying to do and encourage you. It's self-preservation.

I don't worry about failure. I think it's a good thing. It's character building. You fall on your face and feel embarrassed, so what? When you're on the floor there's nowhere else to go but up, and that's a good thing.

You can't be debilitated by your fears. You'll never eliminate them because fear and failure are just part of life, but you don't have to let them paralyse you.

What I've Learned

- You can't change someone else – only yourself

- Life is scary but that is what it means to be alive

- Don't let fear stop you pursuing your dream

- Believe in yourself

Woman to Woman

The day Andreas told me he was having an affair and the girl was pregnant, everything changed.

I knew we were in real trouble.

We both sat crying, utterly devastated. When something that huge drops on you from nowhere, you can't take it in. It's like a bomb going off. You pick your way through the rubble in a state of shock feeling like everything you knew and trusted has been blown to bits. I had no idea what was going to happen next, but in my heart I didn't want him to go, and I didn't think he would.

By then, we'd had five years together and even though we had our problems, we loved each other. We'd built a life together, and I always felt he was committed to me and my daughter, Monet. Deep down, I thought, 'He'll stay, we'll get through this.' I didn't know what I was up against, though, and how far the woman he'd been seeing would go to keep him.

I can't even begin to say how many tears there were. God alone knows how, but we kept things going. We even got closer. Then I found out I was pregnant. That whole period in my life was one of the toughest ever, but I knew I couldn't let it break me. I had no idea what was going to happen, if he was going to leave, make a life with her, or be there for me and our child. I knew I had to take care of myself.

Suddenly I was on a mission, training hard, getting myself into the best shape ever. Throughout my pregnancy I was fit and well. I had so much energy and the stronger I was physically, the better I felt emotionally. Going to the gym saved me. It gave me a purpose, stopped me wallowing and falling apart.

To be honest, I don't know how I'd have coped without it and that's why I always say you have to keep moving, even when you're at your lowest ebb. Just getting up and doing *something* does stop you from going under.

It's true that when you exercise your body, your mind is strong. It doesn't mean you won't feel pain because there's no getting away from it, but you will find a way of coping. I was so hurt and angry with Andreas, but I loved him and I was having his child.

When her baby was born in 2005, I had to let him go to be with his child; she was his responsibility. I thought he was doing the right thing, being a dutiful father. While he was gone it was the most horrible time, absolute hell, but I just kept going, working out, taking care of myself and, just before Christmas, 2005, he came home.

In March 2006, a few weeks before the baby was due he told me he had to go away on business, that he'd be gone a while, but would be back.

That was the last time we were together. I still believed he'd come. but when I went into labour there was no sign of him. Right until the last minute I still thought he'd show up but, just as I was about to give birth, I finally realised he wasn't going to. It was my darkest moment.

Russia, the most beautiful baby girl, the double of her father, came into the world on May 15th, 2006, and, a few minutes later, Andreas finally called. The man I loved and counted on for seven years – my best friend, my everything – was not there when I needed him.

The Other Woman

I don't understand how a woman can get involved with a man when he's already in a relationship. Surely, if you're conscious, if you have a conscience, you can't go there. I know I can't.

I actually think women are in trouble on lots of fronts right now because there are those who have no conscience. Sometimes I think we've totally lost our way and that women are their own worst enemies. Why would you want to be with a man who has someone else anyway? Doesn't the fact he wants to see you on the side and keep you a secret tell you something? Aren't you bothered that he's got a woman he's happy to be seen with and it's not you? Does being the other woman make you feel happy and secure and good about yourself – or a bit sordid? Just what *is* going on?

I don't think anyone can expect to be happy and fulfilled if what drives them is being self-*ish* rather than self-*less*. Being conscious is about doing the right thing, being the best you can be, having respect for every other human being. Basically, there are two types of women: the serious one who's the wife, the one the guy's seen with, and the mistress – the secret, the one hidden away in some hotel room.

No one can tell me any woman feels good about that. A woman who settles for that is saying she doesn't value herself, doesn't think she's anything. As soon as you allow yourself to be number two, second best, you're saying you've got issues with self-worth.

Any woman who thinks that's okay is deluding herself. It's not okay.

Some people see affairs as thrilling, but you don't get the high without the come down. When he doesn't call or show up because he's with his regular chick and you just have to put up with it, how thrilling is that?

I don't believe you can get love and fulfilment from something that's done in secret. I'm not excusing the guy either. Anyone who has an affair is basically saying they don't care. They're only interested in satisfying their needs, regardless of who else gets hurt along the way. And, trust me, someone is always going to get hurt.

What an affair says about you is that you're selfish, that you put lust above anything else, and fulfilling your sexual desires comes before decency and integrity. You can dress it up any way you want, but that's what it comes down to in the end. An affair isn't a relationship; it's about having sex in secret. And I think once you're mature that's not something you want to do. Affairs reek of immaturity.

Have a Good Heart

Sometimes, however much you love someone, you have to admit defeat and move on. Of course it's so hard to see the guy you love leave – and some relationships are definitely worth fighting for – but a love triangle with two women fighting over a man is destructive and humiliating. It's not going to make you feel good, whatever happens in the end. Maybe you'll feel like the loser if he leaves you for another woman, but you will get over it. And once a bit of time goes by, and you can look at things in the cold light of day, you're going to know you did the right thing.

Just try not to focus too much on what's going on when everything is falling apart because that's when you're raw, all over the place emotionally, and nowhere near rational. Yeah, it hurts – it hurts like hell – but when you play it clean you keep your self-respect and your dignity and there's a lot to be said for that.

Make sure your heart is always in the right place, even when you're in bits, and I guarantee you'll win in the end. It might not feel like it right away, but the one with the good heart always wins.

I was talking to a woman recently who'd been through exactly the same thing as me with her partner and she said, 'The woman who holds on tightest wins.' I looked her and I thought, does she? Does she really win? And if she does, what's the prize? A guy who gives in to whoever throws the biggest tantrum? You probably will get to keep him if you shout and scream and threaten because you'll frighten the living crap out of him, but deep down he's not going to like it, and you're not going to feel secure because you'll never know if he really wants to be with you or if he's there because you held a gun to his head. I just think if that's what you have to do to make someone be with you then it's not going to last. It can't. And, the more you put the squeeze on a man who's afraid of intimacy – which is why he had an affair in the first place, remember – the more likely he is to cheat all over again.

I met a woman who'd had an affair and the guy she was seeing left his wife to be with her, settled down, had a couple of kids – then walked out and went back to his ex-wife. They re-married and, 20 years on, they're still together. The mistress, the one who thought she'd won, is still alone and bitter. How a relationship begins is always telling. If it's some hole-in-the-corner thing and the guy is telling lies so he can be with you, you're in trouble.

Revenge is Never Sweet

It's horrible when the guy you love cheats on you. You're heartbroken and your ego takes a kicking. You're going to have times when you want to make him hurt, too, but let it go. That's just the ego wanting payback. I definitely had my moments, but you can't give in to them. You can't let your emotional state take over and control you. When you're hurt and angry the ego's going to be looking for revenge, but don't listen to it. Retribution doesn't work. Focus on taking care of yourself instead.

Love is the most powerful thing in the world. I get more done by being loving than I ever will by being destructive. Forgiveness is the biggest thing you can do. Forgive him *and* forgive her because that's the best thing you can do for *you*.

When *So Good* went platinum the first thing I did was get a disc made and give it to the boyfriend who'd cheated on me. While you're still angry, still hurting, they're getting on with their life. They're probably out having dinner with someone else, not thinking two seconds about you, and there you are at home holding onto the pain. It's counter-productive and you have to stop doing it because it's messing you up, not them.

> Love is the most powerful thing in the world

You think people are laughing at you, thinking you've been a complete idiot, and it hurts. I've come to realise that there's no point worrying what people think. They're always going to have an opinion and that's okay. You don't need to let their opinions crush you. You just have to remember whatever you're going through is the same stuff we all go through. It happens every flipping day of the week and it's nothing to be ashamed of.

I've had it all said about me, awful stuff in the press, but I've learned not to let it eat me up. One week they say, 'Mica's a fat cow,' and the next, 'Mica's gorgeous.' It doesn't matter. People can call you anything they like; what counts is you being true to yourself. You can only be real. Some people are going to like you and others aren't. Learn to appreciate it when you are liked and not obsess about it when you're not. Don't let your feelings take you over.

Instead, ask yourself why you allowed that person into your life in the first place and what you needed to learn from them. That's always the key. Every time you experience pain, it's teaching you something. When you go through agony it's because something in your life has to shift. Pain is gain.

Andreas made me see my stuff. What I went through with him made me look at myself and see what was really going on, why I was making the same mistakes over and over. Forgiveness helps you see the bigger picture.

Unless you forgive, your life is like watching a movie on pause. How frustrating is that when you can't get to see the rest of it? For that reason alone you have to forgive. Anyone who says they can't forgive – well, that says to me they'll never love. Love is the most powerful force there is. It can get you through anything. Love really does conquer all. And forgiveness is part of love. The two go hand in hand. You can't have one without the other.

You have to wonder if you really want to live like that, being angry and hard done by when whoever it is you blame doesn't care anymore. You have to get over it. Think about what it is you're doing here. Do you want to grow and get more interesting? Do you want to have a great life? Well then, you have to go through some hurdles. Life isn't plain sailing.

It takes guts to own up and accept that you created the situation that's just broken you in two. It takes guts to stop blaming everyone else. Taking responsibility isn't always easy. You have to take a long hard look at yourself and think, okay, why did I let him/her/them do that to me? And sometimes you're not going to like the answer. Sometimes you have to admit that you knew exactly what kind of person you were letting in and you went there anyway. You could see what they were about and you still jumped in. I know because that's exactly what I've done in the past.

When you start taking care of your own stuff, that's when you also start to rise. There's nothing holding you down anymore, you're not wasting time blaming someone else for the fact you're not happy, you're busy working out what to do about it. That's when your life starts to change, when you finally realise – 'Oh, I get it – it was *me* all along.'

I Needed That

I don't believe people come into our lives by chance. I think we set things up so that we attract the people we need when we need them. Once you start to think like that, you don't get bitter. Bitterness comes when you get into thinking whatever has gone wrong is someone else's fault and nothing to do with you.

The blame game makes you sit there, broken, waiting for another person to erase the pain they've caused and, when they don't, you feel even worse. You can't afford to be like that because half the time they really don't know what they've done.

You can't let someone who is going through life asleep and unaware ruin your life and make you cynical, so forgive them and move on. Just think how much worse it would be if they were conscious – if they *did* know what they were doing. What you're learning is that the most dangerous human being is the one that's not awake.

Love takes real courage. It's always risky to put your heart on the line, put everything out there, be open to being hurt. You don't know what's going to happen, how painful it might get, but you do it anyway because you believe in love and if it all goes wrong and you end up disappointed and broken-hearted further down the line, it's just a chance you take.

When you're open, out there searching for answers, you've every chance of finding them and when you stop making it all about him and focus on yourself you start to understand why things happen the way they do and you cease to feel bitter.

Just before I was due to give birth to Russia, I decided to get rid of Andreas's stuff. I packed it up, put it in the garage, and got a removals firm to put the whole lot into storage. Looking around, seeing all his things, just made things worse. I didn't want to get rid of it, but I knew I was going to have to for the sake of my own pride and self-esteem. It was horrible, packing his things, emptying drawers, taking his stuff out of the wardrobe. I hated doing it and the whole time I cried like a baby. There was no way I was going to try to keep him if he wanted someone else. I'm not needy like that. Love isn't about control. It's not about tying someone down. Love is about free will.

I've worked so hard to get to where I am and feel good about myself that I couldn't let him or her, or anybody, take it away. In the end, as much as I loved him, I had to put myself first.

I told him, 'I love you dearly, but she can have you. She clearly needs you more than I do.' When she called, I said, 'Take him and good luck on your quest.' I haven't spoken to her since.

Flush Out the Toxins

Anything toxic in your life is going to poison your system. You might not even be aware of what those toxins are and the damage they're doing.

Toxicity comes in many forms.

- Images of anorexic women that make us feel we've got to be skinny to be beautiful are toxic.
- Junk food filled with additives and fat is toxic.
- Spending hours in front of the TV watching mindless stuff is toxic.
- Jealousy is toxic.
- Self-loathing is toxic.
- Drinking to oblivion is toxic.
- Drugs are toxic.
- Depression is toxic.
- Selfishness is toxic.
- Relationships that drag you down are toxic.

Even when we have a pretty good idea what's bad for us, we don't necessarily know what to do about it. Sometimes we don't actually want to do anything because we're hooked. It's really easy to get into bad habits: eating too much, disappearing into a bottle at the end of the day, sticking with someone even though we know they make us feel like crap. It becomes a pattern, familiar, and we get used to it. We even get to like it.

Dealing with toxic stuff isn't easy. If it was nobody would be eating rubbish or getting wasted on drink and drugs or tolerating destructive relationships. So, why do we do it?

It always comes back to self-worth, to having a goal, a dream, something to attain. Things change for the better when you get into the habit of putting *you* first, acknowledging your value, investing time and energy in your emotional and physical and spiritual health, knowing your purpose in life.

That's not being selfish – it's about being the best you can be, and that benefits everyone. Once you have a purpose the toxic stuff becomes secondary anyway. Having a purpose makes you forget about obsessive eating, obsessive drinking, abusive relationships, or whatever it is you're doing, because you have a goal. You're thinking, 'I know where I want to go and I know I have to be healthy and fit to get there so I'm going to make sure I don't abuse myself.'

When you don't have a goal you compensate by over-eating, over-drinking, over-shopping to fill a void. You have to learn to recognise self-abuse, in whatever form it takes, as a sign you're not fulfilling your potential at some level. That's always what it's about.

When you have a higher purpose, a passion, you don't want to drink your life away, ruin your liver and wreck your health, because you've got too much great stuff going on. Have a drink, just don't get drunk. Drink for pleasure, not to fall down and vomit and lose all sense of control. There's a difference between having a drink and the drink having you.

Why go through the feelings of guilt and self-hatred from feeding your body rubbish? Why not just avoid the whole gorge and purge, gorge and purge thing in the first place? It's about striking a balance. Every now and then you're going to want what I call a piece of lard – a doughnut, a bag of chips – just make it a treat for once a week, not something you have every day. It's about balance and moderation. Whatever you do, just don't *over*-do it.

Adapt the mentality of an athlete and be disciplined. Be focused on whatever it is you want to achieve and accept that to succeed you need to be fit and well.

What's Your Poison?

One of the hardest changes I made was to stop smoking. I loved my fags.
I started smoking when I was 17 and stopped about three years ago, and I *still*
have moments when I'd love a fag. I'll even sit next to people who smoke just
because I love the smell of it. It's a really bad vice for me. The worst thing
about cigarettes is you never get over the craving.

I got a wake-up call, though, when smoking started affecting my voice.
I could feel it cracking and I was losing my top note. I knew something wasn't
right and it turned out I had a cyst on my vocal cords. I was told that if I kept
on smoking I'd lose my voice. That was it. I tried giving up on my own, gave
the nicotine patches a go, but nothing worked so I went to a hypnotherapist
who asked me on a scale of 1-10 how serious I was about giving up. I said 8.
Three sessions later I was off the fags.

They reckon nicotine is as addictive as heroin and it's definitely a hard
habit to break, but I was ready to stop. I was already asking myself why I was
smoking but, on my own, I was struggling to give up. I think you really have
to get to that place where you've had enough. Just look at people with
smoking-related illnesses if you need a reason to give up.

Once I'd stopped I felt so much better and my chest was clear for the first
time in years. Food started tasting good, but then my weight ballooned and
I got really big. I was heading for a size 18 and knew I had to get to work and
do something about it. Basically, I'd replaced the cigarettes with food, so I
had to take a hard look at what I was eating and how much training I was
doing. That just made me realise you have to be conscious of your body, be
aware when it changes, and understand what's going on.

No Smoke Without . . . Wrinkles

We all know smoking is bad for us. It's the biggest single cause of cancer in
the world. Something like 45,000 people in the UK die from smoking-related

cancers every year and if that doesn't make you want to stop, maybe how cigarettes affect your looks will.

The best thing about giving up smoking was that my skin just started glowing. Smoking is one of the worst things you can do to your skin. It robs it of oxygen and essential nutrients, including vitamin C. Basically, if you smoke you're depriving your skin of the things it needs most to be healthy, and fast-forwarding the ageing process. Smoking gives you a grey, tired pallor. And all that dragging on cigarettes gives you wrinkles around the eyes and the mouth. Researchers believe it breaks down collagen in the skin, which you need for elasticity. So the more you smoke, the more likely you are to get wrinkles and end up with skin that looks 20 years older than it actually is – and no beauty product is going to be able to do a thing about it.

Bad Habits

When I look at what's going on in London, it's awash with drugs, particularly cocaine, which people call 'recreational', as if that means it's okay. It's terrible out there, everyone running from themselves, getting high, afraid of what they might see if they actually stopped to look at who they really are. They might actually like what they see, but they're too busy running away to find out. Cocaine is such a dark drug and it's scary what it does to people, how it can turn someone from Jekyll into Hyde in an instant.

I was only 17 when I was making my first album, and cocaine was everywhere. The only thing was I didn't realise it. I couldn't understand why some of the people I was really close to acted the way they did. They'd say one thing and do another. This went on all the time, deception, lies – and no one cared. The only person who was bothered was me. All the time they were snorting coke and me (so flipping green) had no idea.

I've seen what coke does to people – the mood swings, the erratic behaviour – and, believe me, there's nothing recreational about it. It's the kind of drug you might start taking once a week, then twice a week, until you can't do without it and it's messing you up. People who take coke become dark and cold and selfish. That's a real mark of cocaine. It makes people so self-obsessed they have no thought for anyone but themselves.

I know people who say, 'I wouldn't know how to go out without a line.'

I just think we have to get back to that place where we know how to have fun without being intoxicated. Enjoying yourself doesn't have to mean getting high or getting hammered. We have to enjoy our lives without wanting to destroy our lives.

I went to a party a few months back and I knew as soon as I walked in it was off-key, that there was a bad energy in the place because everyone in there was coking it. The place was poisonous. I actually love going out and meeting people, I'm a real party girl – I mean I put the S in sociable – but I was absolutely bored. Everyone was talking utter crap at each other, all this me me me stuff, and *nobody* was engaging. It's like they're not really with you so you end up thinking, 'I might as well not be here.' I turned to the girl who was with me and said, 'I've got to get out of here, I just can't do it,' so we left. What really bothered me was that those people were all wealthy and all they're doing with their money is taking drugs. They could be out there helping people, doing something positive, being charitable. There's a million and one ways they could spend their money and there they are, week in, week, out, getting high. It's really depressing.

Constructive Giving

Getting the balance right isn't always easy, but it's crucial to everything you do. I think a lot of women struggle with balance when it comes to giving. They give and give and give until there's nothing left. Healthy giving isn't about making others feel good at your own expense – it's also about you.

I've definitely been guilty of over-giving in the past, putting everyone else first, over-extending myself. It's something I've done in all of my relationships and it really doesn't work. What happens is you end up depleted. The relationship becomes all about what you can do for the other person and nothing to do with your own growth and fulfilment.

I think a lot of women do that, make the guy they're with all-important, sometimes without knowing it, sometimes only realising when it's too late. They see their role as nurturing and supportive and generous – and there's nothing wrong with that, as long as it's not all one-way traffic.

When you carry another person it's the most exhausting, debilitating thing. It doesn't matter whether you're carrying them financially or emotionally or spiritually – you end up so weighed down, so focused on them, that you neglect yourself.

The irony is you think you're helping them, but you're not because as long as you carry the load you're screwing up their chance of taking responsibility for their own stuff. And taking responsibility is something we all have to do. I don't say we can't be generous and giving in the relationships we have. I just think we have to get it right, make sure it's a healthy thing, because when it's one-sided it becomes damaging.

You might think you can handle it but, in the long run, when one person is doing all the giving and the other is doing all the taking, it breeds resentment and misery. It makes you question the whole basis of what you have together.

Relationships shouldn't be tiring. They shouldn't tax you. They should be exhilarating. If you feel weighed down by the person you're with, the chances are you're doing all the work.

The best relationships aren't a struggle. They're about mutual exchange and empowerment. Once you put your own health and emotional well-being first, you're less likely to take on someone else's problems. You have your own stuff and dealing with that takes priority. It has to, because only you can fix you.

If there's a guy out there broken, a mess, he's going to have to deal with that himself. You can offer support, encouragement, but in a detached way. You can't get in there and start trying to make things right.

We can only make it right for ourselves.

It doesn't matter if you can see what's wrong and exactly what needs fixing – forget it. It's a waste of time. Why help someone when they're not going to make use of it? You have to plant seeds in fertile ground if you want something to grow. I think we have to be more constructive with how we give.

The more you take care of yourself, the stronger you become, and the more aware you are, the better you'll be at seeing the guys that are broken and needy, and when the prospect of rescuing someone, making things better for them, fixing them, ceases to be appealing you'll know you're making progress.

Learning from Love

It's easy to be judgmental about other people's relationships, to think they're crazy for even going there, to feel superior. I've had all that said about me. So what? I've made mistakes, fallen in love with guys who've turned out to be complete arseholes, had my heart broken, done the same thing all over again. And you know what – it's fine.

If you'd walked into my house in the months after I split up with Andreas you'd have found a copy of *The DNA of Relationships* in my bedroom. I was trying to understand what went wrong – and work out how not to do the same thing again. Just trying to find a solution is incredibly powerful and stops your feelings from getting stuck in a destructive rut.

In the end, every relationship teaches you something. When I was much younger I fell in love with a guy, thought we had something good, believed we could make a life together, but he had a temper and when he lost it he'd throw things, smash the place up. Some women might have been out of there like a shot. I stayed, though, because I loved him and I really wanted to make it work. I didn't just want to walk away; I'd made a commitment and I was in it for the long haul.

I also think it's not always the right thing to walk away at the first sign of trouble. Sometimes, when there's a will on both sides, relationships can survive even the most appalling difficulties.

His anger turned out to be poisonous, though, out of control and totally destructive as far as our relationship was concerned. I could just about deal with seeing my house – and things I'd worked hard for – smashed to pieces, but one day it went beyond that and he hit me.

I got home a bit later than he expected, and he was furious, convinced I'd been with someone else. All I'd actually been doing was shopping and I had the bags to prove it, but he didn't believe me. We rowed and he slapped my face. It's the only time a man has hit me. That was it. I was out of the door.

Some women don't leave, though. They stay, tolerate the violence, blame themselves, and try to make things right. Basically, they're trapped by their own sense of low self-worth, and all the time the problems they're going through are making them feel worse and more helpless.

Of course a relationship doesn't have to be violent to be deemed abusive. Abuse comes in many different forms. Some of the most awful men use emotional tactics to batter women. It's more subtle, but just as effective. And, sometimes, when there's a steady *drip drip drip* of poison seeping into your veins every day it takes longer to come to your senses and work out what's really going on. All I'd say is whenever the person you're with makes you feel crap, they're not right for you. That still doesn't mean it's easy to walk away. It's that thing of stepping out of familiar territory, starting again and it can take a huge amount of courage.

The Game

Falling in love, opening up your heart to another person, is a real act of courage and not everyone can do it. There are a lot of people out there too afraid to love. They're looking for 'safe' love, love at a distance, without commitment or any real sense of attachment. Safe love isn't love at all.

Real love says I might get hurt, broken, left for dead, but, guess what, it's not going to finish me off. I can get up and move on. What makes you strong is the ability to feel, to be hurt, to be kicked right, left and centre, and *still* get back up. It's about going there knowing you might have your heart ripped to shreds because you have the courage to love. It's the biggest thing you can do.

It's amazing how people play games when it comes to relationships. You get the ones who call and text and then the minute you show an interest back off. It's a game and it's not worth going there. If someone is doing that, just get out because they're playing with you.

People who have nothing to hide put their cards on the table. If they're keeping something back, what's that telling you? The person looking for safe love is seeking to create relationships where they don't have to reveal their true feelings. It's about concealment, not openness. Safe love is shifty. Do you want to be a part of that?

The problem is that, usually, we're attracted to what we know, to whatever we were taught love is, and that's why we get involved with people who are playing games. I was taught to love my dad from a distance. He would turn up and then he'd be gone. He was the visitor.

When we attract someone who wants to play games, we have to try and work out why. What makes someone get involved with a person who makes them feel miserable and insecure, who calls, then pulls away, blows hot and cold all the time?

Real love doesn't make you feel anxious, insecure and fearful

Usually, it's because they went through that same thing with a parent or some other authority figure when they were growing up – which is why they attract the game player in the first place, and why the attraction is so powerful.

It can be a long time before you wake up and work out what's going on and that's when you see that the person who did that to you all those years ago had their own problems, that *they* didn't know how to love properly, so that's what they taught you, and now you're doing the same thing. The cycle just goes on and on.

Not everyone wants real love. Some people are quite happy to play the game. They associate love with deception and concealment because that's what they know. That's their truth. What you have to ask is – why is it your truth? Why are you accepting a version of love that's broken and screwed up and damaging?

Is it because you don't feel good enough?

Is it because 'the game' is fun and unpredictable and you're frightened life would be boring if you didn't have that uncertainty, the not knowing if he's going to call, if he's really into you? Or, is it because that's what you were taught?

- Real love doesn't make you feel anxious, insecure and fearful.
- Real love isn't being with someone who leaves a cute message on your phone, then ignores your calls.
- Real love isn't about being picked up and dropped when someone else feels like it, or held at arm's length, or made to wonder where the hell you stand. That's not love – that's manipulation.
- Real love goes something like this:
  'I really like you, can I meet you?'
  'Yeah, I'd like that.'
  'Can you do five o'clock?'
  'Yeah, that would be good.'
  'Great, I can't wait to see you.'
  'I can't wait to see you, too.'
  Simple, straightforward, no playing games. Learn the signs.

Not My Type

When you repeat the same destructive patterns for years, having one bad relationship after another, never quite seeing what's going wrong and your part in it, it means you're still learning.

Then, suddenly, the guys you've always fallen for, the ones you're never happy with, stop being attractive. You start to see them for what they are.

I was at a party a few months ago and I met this guy, definitely the type I'd usually go for, and what was really weird was that I was standing there watching him work me. It was like I was an observer and I could see exactly what was going on. Usually I'm right there, buying it, doing it – being part of 'the game'. Not anymore. I'm so sick and tired of that type, totally exhausted. Flash just doesn't appeal to me now.

Realising that was the kick up the backside I needed to get my life moving. Everything started to happen for me as soon as Andreas and I broke up. That was the catalyst for change and without it I'd still be sat in that damned relationship putting on weight, feeling more miserable every day.

When we broke up it took me four months to sit down and send him an email to say, 'You really hurt me, broke me in pieces, and I've had a hard time forgiving you, but we have a wonderful baby together so let's try to be good role models.'

I can't hate the guy. I can't be jealous of the girl he's with. I fell in love with him, and I know that underneath it all he's a good person, and that he'll find his way. We can be friends, but in the end we're on a different journey.

There's Only One You

We live in such a competitive age with everyone trying to outdo each other, always go one better, and that leads to two things: we fail to appreciate our own unique qualities and we get jealous of the people we see doing better than us.

Most people know what it is to feel pangs of jealousy, even if they don't admit to it. No one wants to own up to being jealous because it's such a dark and negative emotion. When someone's jealous of you, they will seek to destroy you. They don't just want what you've got, they want to be you – and that means one of you is going to have to go.

It's usually the people closest to us who are the most jealous of us, the ones who say, 'You know, I don't think you should wear that, it doesn't do anything for you,' or, 'Oh - what have you done to your hair?'

It's psychological warfare to erode your confidence and it will slowly start to break you down.

Sometimes those digs are so subtle you don't even see them. You just start feeling a bit low, a bit unsure, so you keep looking for reassurance, and the friend who is jealous keeps on attacking, firing those poison arrows, undermining your self-worth.

Some people actually liked the fact you didn't look good and when they see you getting into shape, dropping the weight, getting that healthy glow, they want to put you right back in the place you were before. They feel threatened.

When you are criticised, don't react. When other people feed you negative opinions, don't react. Don't be offended by criticism, turn it to your advantage. Just sit there and be cool. Tell yourself it hurts, but it's okay.

Criticism is good because it gives you humility and, when someone gives you a kick, it's an incentive to find the energy and power to do better.

The best thing you can do – and this is a big one – is feel compassion for the person who had a go because I guarantee that when someone criticises you it's because they're feeling bad about themselves.

Being human means there are going to be times when you will feel insecure and jealous of somebody else – you just don't have to let those feelings control you. The way to deal with it is to recognise that the person you're jealous of is just having their moment and yours hasn't come – yet. Just because they're having success, doesn't mean you won't.

When you see the bigger picture you're aware that there's room for everyone and that as long as you have a purpose and a passion your time will come. You're still going to experience those pangs of jealousy, but you'll be able to put them in their place and know that regardless of how well anyone else is doing things will work out for you, too.

It's about appreciating your individual talents and having a strong sense of who you are and what you can do. Fall in love with the gift you have. If that's where you're coming from, you won't feel threatened by anyone else. Once you understand you're unique, that no one sings the way you do, or writes the way you do, or does anything the way you do, you stop feeling jealous. We're all different, that's all.

That's why it's so important to be true to yourself, to always express the real you, and to create something unique. Be inspired and influenced by others, but don't try to be them. There's only one Corinne Bailey Rae, only one Britney Spears, only one Diana Ross. There's only one *you*, and fulfilling your potential means cultivating the *true* you.

We all have it in us to be amazing, but most people aren't encouraged to think like that. It starts in childhood. If you encourage children, push them and make them believe in themselves, they can become giants. Praise and encouragement builds confidence and produces kids that believe they're worth something. You just have to watch and see what a child is good at and push them to focus on their strengths.

> It's about appreciating your individual talents and having a strong sense of who you are and what you can do

There's no point telling someone to do A when they're good at B. Encourage them to concentrate on what they do best. When my daughter, Russia, started standing up I'd clap and say, 'Good girl!' Every time she got to her feet she'd look to me for encouragement and just that little bit of praise and enthusiasm would make her so pleased with herself. We're all like that.

When I was growing up in Lewisham, south London, dreaming of being a singer, all my friends told me I'd never make it. They couldn't see my dream. I left them all behind and went to live with my sister in Brixton. Suddenly everything started happening. I was doing backing vocals for bands like Hollywood Beyond and Shakatak and then, when I was 17, I got my deal with Island Records.

If you grow up without receiving praise, you're not going to have a strong sense of self-belief. You're going to feel mediocre because you've never been told anything different. *Nobody* is mediocre. Tell yourself that every day. We all have unique strengths and abilities and, if we want to have great lives, we have to work out what they are and play to them.

Change

You have to be focused. You can't let toxic stuff get in the way. That's why there's no room for negative people. I have a friend who calls me and says, 'I'm feeling really low,' and I say, 'Why? Don't be.' We all have choices.

If there's someone in your life who enjoys being a victim, loves offloading their stuff onto you, you can't entertain it, otherwise you'll end up just like them. They say, 'I hate my job, I hate my life, everything's shit,' and you just have to say one thing back – 'Change.' That's it. If someone doesn't like what's going on, *change* it.

There are people who like being victims, people whose purpose in life is to continue to play the victim role, and they're looking to you to reinforce it. Every time you let them offload on you, you're becoming a victim, too. Their problems mess you up and bring you down.

If you love someone like that you have to be curt and cut them off to help them. Don't try to tell them where they're going wrong, just live your life in a way that shows them there's another way. Lead by example; people are always more influenced by what you do than what you say.

When you aid and abet them in their misery, all you're doing is stopping them from growing and poisoning your own system at the same time.

Ask yourself why you put up with someone who never makes you feel good. Is it because you're scared of being on your own? Once you start to like your own company, the idea of being alone isn't so frightening, so feel the pain of separation and trust that what will follow will be better and more fulfilling.

You have to surround yourself with positive people. Anyone negative has to go. Never mind if you've known them 20 years, if they make you feel like crap, they must go because it's a scientific fact that if you put a positive and negative charge together the positive becomes negative.

You will definitely know in your heart the people who make you feel good and the ones who don't, the people who want to see things happen for you and the ones who enjoy seeing you on your face.

You'll have your moments of fear, when you feel unsure and insecure, when you wobble and slip and lose your way. That's going to happen however focused you are. We all feel like that. It's not the end of the world. Just get up and get busy again.

The way I look at it, we're all here to do something serious. I believe that every one of us can make a difference to the world because everything we do creates a ripple that touches other people. I think we all have amazing power and that it's up to us to use it.

When I get to the end of my life I want to be able to look back and know I did some great things – caused a wave, made a difference. Being aware, working on yourself, gives you a sense of urgency and stops you from taking things for granted. It doesn't make you immune to the toxic stuff but it means you become better at handling it, and know how to limit your exposure. Having a great relationship with yourself and the universe gives you the means to do that.

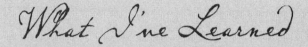

What I've Learned

• The good heart always wins

• Pain teaches us more about ourselves

• Make an effort to be the best you can, because that benefits everyone

• Don't give in to jealousy – your moment will come

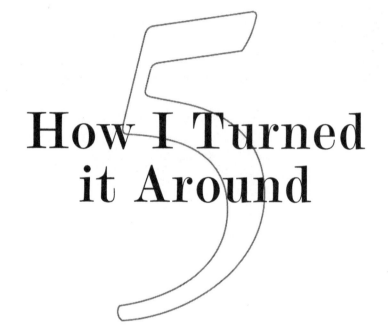

How I Turned
it Around

I never used to think about my weight when I was younger.

I was tall and thin, a bit of a geek really; people used to call me Bony M or Big Bird, like the character in *Sesame Street*. I could eat what I liked – pizza, burgers, you name it – and I was still a skinny rake.

Then I hit 20, my body changed, and I started getting bigger. The weight began to creep on while I was working on my second album, *Contribution*. I put on almost two stone, (which was a lot for someone who'd always been so thin), went up a couple of dress sizes, and got really curvy.

Weight wasn't an issue when the first album, *So Good*, was released. It was a massive hit, went platinum, and everything went crazy. I was running about, promoting my stuff, doing interviews – TV, radio, the lot. You get so caught up in the whole cycle of promotion and it's such a rush that half the time you don't eat, don't even think about eating, so you're definitely not worrying about your weight. The chances are you actually lose weight.

Then, once it all calms down and you start thinking about the next album, you have more time to yourself again. You're in demand, but in a different way. Everyone wants to reward you for the success you've had, treat you, take you out to the best restaurants, and suddenly you're eating out all the time. I was really enjoying all that, going out with record company executives, everyone patting me on the back, telling me I was great. I was eating like a mad person and at the same time my life had slowed down, so of course my weight started to go up. I'd been a size 10, but all of a sudden I was buying size 14 clothes.

One day an important person at the record company called me in. He said, 'Mica, you've got to lose weight. You look like two people in one body.'

I was devastated, really hurt, but I made up my mind that the extra pounds were coming off.

That was the first time I tried a crash diet. I starved myself, picked at food here and there, more or less stopped eating, got by on coffee and cigarettes, and the weight dropped off. I'd go to the steam room and sit there for ages sweating it all out. It was nuts, just rubbish, and I felt like crap, but I got really thin and everyone thought I looked great.

I was miserable, though, living on my nerves, fed-up, stressed-out – and starving. It didn't take much to make me lose my temper. I was on edge all the time, my nerves were raw, and every little thing would get to me. My hair even fell out because my body wasn't getting the nutrients it needed.

It was madness but I know I'm not the only woman to have crash dieted. I'd say many women have, at some stage, gone to extreme lengths to lose weight. For many, dieting is a way of life.

After years of starving myself, losing weight, then finding as soon as I stop it all goes back on – and more besides – I've learned that *diets don't work*.

What's Eating You?

I struggled with my weight for years, until I finally worked out where I was going wrong and decided I was never going to diet again. I don't want to punish my body anymore. I actually want to take care of it, and that doesn't mean killing myself to be a size 10.

I'm not skinny anymore, but I *am* in the best shape I've ever been. I'm 5' 11", a healthy size 14, sometimes a 16, and I love my body. No way am I meant to be a size 10.

There's something really nice about being fit and healthy. In the past I've been way too thin and I've also gone the other way, let myself go, and got too big.

What I've discovered is that if you focus on *health* rather than *weight*, your body ends up the size it's meant to be. When your goal is about being healthy, everything starts to fall into place and you can be the right size *for you* without counting calories, without depriving your body of food, without hurting yourself.

All I've done is make a few basic changes to the way I live. I believe in eating well, drinking lots of water, taking regular, moderate exercise. I've found that being consistent and disciplined in whatever you do is half the battle and that there's definitely no such thing as a short-cut. If you want to feel and look your best, you have to be prepared to do the work and be in there for the long haul.

What I'm advocating is a programme for life, something straightforward and manageable. You'll definitely see results, but you do have to put your mind to it.

You Have to Want to Change

The first step has to be a real desire to change. You have to be ready and willing to start taking care of yourself, and the best way to send that signal to your body is by doing something practical. You have to let your body know you're serious about making changes.

Four years ago I was going to the gym, working out, but I wasn't seeing any progress and it was really frustrating. Back then, I was maybe a couple of stones heavier than I am now, not feeling great, wanting to get into good shape, but not seeing results. I didn't understand why my body wasn't changing when I was doing all that work. All I could think was that maybe I wasn't eating the right stuff, so I went to a nutritionist and she got me to make an inventory of everything I ate over the next week. I'd never done that before and it really made me think about exactly what I was eating. Sometimes just stepping back and taking stock can be rewarding.

The biggest problem for me was I was eating far too much rice, having white rice almost every day, and my body didn't like it. The nutritionist told me to cut it out and to steer clear of white bread and pasta, too. Basically I was having too much starch, too much heavy food, the wrong kind of carbohydrates. If I eat pasta, rice, bread – any kind of refined carbs – my body blows up like a balloon, and that's what was going on.

I loved all that stuff, especially rice, the sticky kind, which is the worst, and it was really clogging up my body. So although I was training, because I was eating the wrong food I wasn't seeing a difference.

My body actually likes protein more than carbohydrates, so it's better for me to eat steamed fish and chicken and get my carbs from vegetables. I know now that when it comes to carbs I have to eat the right kind. I stopped eating white bread and switched to rye instead – the only kind of bread I eat these days – and cut right down on rice. That's when I started to see a change.

Starchy food makes me feel uncomfortable and heavy, like I've just swallowed a person. When I eat that stuff all I want to do afterwards is go to bed. I don't say cut out carbs completely but make them good carbs – fruit, veg, whole grains – and see if it makes a difference to you.

I don't advocate never eating certain foods again, but I try to limit anything that doesn't suit me. It's about moderation, having less of the stuff you know your body is going to struggle with. If you're in a fantastic Italian restaurant, of course it's okay to eat pasta. If you love Indian food, have your chicken curry and rice, but have it once a week, not every night.

Eating the right stuff and eating well is all about getting the balance right *for you*. Some Caribbean foods, like sweet potatoes and green bananas, are great for me but if I eat rice and peas and chicken, which is also a very Jamaican thing, I make sure I have a big portion of chicken and just a spoonful of the rice, and I only eat like that once in a while.

Your body gets used to different food; it gets to like what's good for it, and so do you. Once you know what's not working, you don't actually want to eat it anymore. It's about being conscious of what you're putting into your body and how it makes you feel.

I used to take sugar in my tea, just one spoonful, which doesn't sound like a lot, but when you add it up over a week, two or three cups of tea a day, you'd be surprised how much you get through. I used to have honey, thinking it was healthy – until the nutritionist told me that's sugar as well. So, out went the sugar and the honey, and I felt the difference right away.

If you're getting a healthy, balanced diet, your body is going to get all the sugar it needs. There's no need to add sugar to your food. Refined sugar has no nutritional value whatsoever in terms of vitamins, minerals, or trace elements. It's just calories and eating too much has been linked to mood swings. If you really can't do without it, cut down. Have half a spoon instead of a whole one. Those small adjustments are worth making.

Once you get past 30, your body becomes a bit sluggish and the kind of food you've been eating in the past might not be right for you anymore. If you're still eating the way you always have, but are getting bigger it's your body's way of saying it's time to make some changes.

The reason I like the way I eat now is because I actually feel good after a meal, my body feels light, not like it wants to collapse.

Water

The other big change I made after seeing a nutritionist was to drink more water. I never used to bother, maybe have a glass a week, if that, but she told me to make a habit of drinking two litres a day, and it's something I stick to now. I carry my bottle of water round with me and by the end of the day it's gone.

Keeping the body hydrated is a massive part of feeling good. It's easy to confuse thirst with hunger, so what you find when you're drinking enough water is you don't actually want to eat as much.

Having enough water is essential for good health. It's the one bit of advice none of us can afford to ignore. Our bodies are made up of around 70 per cent water and unless we're properly hydrated we don't function well. Dehydration can cause headaches, lack of energy, and poor concentration – just a dip of one per cent in the water content of the body can be enough to have an adverse effect.

We lose water all the time when we sweat and go to the toilet and we have to keep replacing it. Water is important for digestion, it helps flush out waste and toxins, and it keeps skin looking good.

I can always tell when people aren't drinking enough water because their skin has that dry, lifeless look about it. Keeping a bottle of water with you and getting into the habit of drinking two litres a day will change how you look and feel.

Seeking Advice

What that visit to the nutritionist did was made me conscious of what I eat and that's vital if you want to see your body start to change for the better. Once you start to have that awareness, to think before you eat, you're less likely to eat the wrong food. You're less likely to want bad food and much more likely to choose food that's good for you because you're aware of what your body likes and you want to take care of it. Eating rubbish stops being an option.

I think everyone can benefit from seeing a nutritionist. Just making the decision to get some practical advice sets the ball rolling towards better health and a better body. When you take that conscious step, the mind sends a signal to the body that you're looking after it, that you want it to be well.

The act of going to see someone who can help you is the first positive sign that you're changing the way you think and that alone will start to influence how your body feels. Just making the appointment, going to seek advice, doing something, makes an impact. It's all connected.

Make Friends with Food

Food is amazing. I love food, love to eat, but I only eat healthy stuff. I've trained myself not to like bad food so these days if I eat a burger it doesn't taste real to me. It's like eating plastic, and why in God's name would you want to do that?

Weight is a huge obsession for women, but it needn't be. *Food* should be the obsession – *good* food. When you start being obsessed with eating only good food your weight will never be out of control and you'll never need to think about dieting again. It's important to learn to love food, not make an enemy of it. Diets offer a quick-fix, not a long-term solution. If you really want to get into good shape, and stay in good shape, then you need to look at your lifestyle and that means learning to love food.

I've had this conversation with my daughter, Monet, who's 15. When she talks to me about dieting I say, 'You know what, you can do it but what's going to happen is you'll end up bigger than before. All you're doing is cheating your body and that can't work.'

Diets aren't natural, you can't maintain them, you're just starving yourself and, eventually, you can't do it anymore. You cave in and end up putting all the weight you lost back on, plus more on top. If you eat properly and your body knows it's always going to be fed, it doesn't go into starvation mode and start storing fat.

If you want your body to be lean and fit it's not about losing 10 pounds in 10 days, or whatever diet you want to follow, it's about changing the way you live and eat forever. You have to understand how it works. Forget the quick-fix. It's just cheating.

I say to my daughter, 'You brush your teeth every day and you wouldn't ever think about not bothering for a few weeks, would you?' She goes, 'Oh mum, that's gross, no way.'

That's the way you have to be with food – you have to eat well every day of your life *forever*. Yes, you can have treats now and then, as long as you keep a balance and for 90 per cent of the time stick to good food. Have that bar of chocolate if you want it, but only once in a while. Make healthy eating as much a part of your daily routine as cleaning your teeth – a good habit.

Start Cooking

I love cooking. Everyone in my family cooks – my mum, my dad, everyone – and we all cook really good food. It's a Caribbean thing and it's an important part of life. I was brought up by my grandparents and we always sat down to proper meals together, that's just how it was. I'm still very much that way, cooking, sitting down with my mum, my kids, my sister, all of us eating together.

I think one of the problems we've got today is that so many people don't cook anymore or sit down to eat as a family. They say they don't have time, that it's easier to stick a ready meal in the oven, or whatever. Everyone in the household is eating different food at different times, grabbing something and eating it on the run rather than sitting at the table.

When I was living in America, none of my girlfriends cooked, not one. They'd look at me and say, 'Oh my God, are you cooking? That's amazing!' What they did was order in or eat out – all the time – and to me that was amazing because they had no real connection with the food they ate. From what I can see, that's why there is an unhealthy relationship with food.

If you're not cooking, getting into food, developing a healthy appreciation for what you eat, then how can you be eating well? A lot of the women I meet who have weight problems don't cook and that's the problem. The other problem is we're bringing up our kids to have an unhealthy relationship with food.

You have to educate your kids about food and teach them not to have a problem with it, and it's not easy when we're bombarded with junk food everywhere we turn. What I'm saying is teach your kids to love their food, but make sure it's the right food. I get really upset when I see people eating rubbish – food containing barely any nutrients.

Be aware of what you're putting into your mouth. Be conscious of everything you eat and your relationship with food will start to improve. People who eat like they're shovelling cement in have no love or appreciation for food.

I go to Italy a lot and what I love about the Italians is that eating is a sensual experience for them. They absolutely adore their food, and they take their time over it, really savouring every mouthful. They sit down and eat as a family and their meals aren't rushed. You see it all over Europe – families eating together, appreciating the food, taking their time over it, enjoying the whole experience.

When I was growing up, dinner was the most important meal of the day. We'd all sit at the table together, talk, just have that time together, which was essential in terms of creating unity. In my grandparents' house that's just how it was.

The food that was on the table was always good. We'd eat, and only then would we have something to drink, then we'd all wash up our own dishes. Everyone did their bit. After we'd eaten, the kitchen door would be shut and we wouldn't be allowed in. There was no snacking in between meals. It was hardcore, but it was about being disciplined around food and that stands you in good stead.

When all children are being fed is fish fingers thrown on the grill, or whatever, it can create separation. If kids aren't getting cooked meals at home and don't have a sense of family or being nurtured, they will look for their family unit outside, which probably means heading straight down to the local chippy, eating rubbish, and hanging out on the street in a gang.

I'm not saying everyone has the time to cook every night, but even if it's three times a week or whatever, just try to make it part of your family life. If you have a good relationship with food your kids will, too, and if you all sit down to eat together at the end of the day, you'll have a happier, more unified family.

The reason there are so many kids on the streets messing up is because their home life is fractured. It's up to parents to make home the place their children want to come back to, so that on a winter's day they come in and smell good food and know that's where their creature comforts are, that's where they're safe, that all the good things they've got within the home mean what's outside isn't so great anymore. We have to enforce family time, teach our kids the value of family, and make the home the anchor.

Small Adjustments, Big Benefits

If I eat what works for me, I can have what I like, I never go hungry, and I never have to count calories. If I want a big breakfast, it'll be poached eggs on rye toast with a couple of rashers of grilled bacon and some cherry tomatoes. That's still good food because nothing is fried, but if you really can't live without a fry-up limit it to once a week.

I keep my food simple – steamed veg, roast or baked chicken and fish, and I use fresh herbs, lemon and garlic for seasoning, and olive oil instead of butter. For lunch I might have fish with veg, then a piece of chicken with a massive helping of broccoli or kale for dinner.

I love my greens and I eat lots of kale, a curly, leafy vegetable packed with good stuff like beta-carotene and Vitamin C. There's more Vitamin C in a serving of kale than there is in spinach or carrots. It's a great source of antioxidants, which we need to fight free-radicals that cause disease and ageing. Kale is a good source of calcium, iron, magnesium and potassium and rich in sulphur phytochemicals, which may protect against some types of cancer. It's an excellent source of lutein, which helps prevent age-related macular degeneration – the biggest cause of loss of vision in the UK. I steam kale with garlic, onions, and black pepper, and have it with truffle oil – it tastes wicked.

Salt

If you want to lose weight, you should definitely cut down on salt. Even if you're not adding salt to your food, you're probably getting more than you realise because it's in almost everything we eat, especially processed foods.

The body needs sodium to help maintain body fluids at the correct levels, but when we have too much we retain too much water and gain weight. An excess of salt has been linked to high blood pressure, heart disease and strokes. We need around 6g of salt a day, but the average intake is 9–10g. Most of it comes from processed foods and from adding salt during cooking and at the table. You need to watch foods like bread and breakfast cereals, because they can also be high in salt.

To cut down, stop adding salt to food, eat fresh food rather than processed, and have more fruit and vegetables because the potassium content helps balance the effect of salt on the body. Use a steamer for vegetables instead of boiling them, so the nutrients stay in the food, rather than ending up in the cooking water.

If you buy processed foods, read the label – even healthy-sounding food can contain 'hidden' salt. Bear in mind that sometimes labels only give the sodium content. To work out how much salt there is, multiply sodium by two and a half.

I really think we have to work on our relationship with food, get into the habit of cooking, and steer clear of food that's full of additives and E-numbers. Don't count on processed food to give you the nutrients you need. It might fill you up, but being full doesn't mean being well-fed.

Make a food inventory and really think about what you're putting into your body. Become conscious.

Whatever you do, try not to develop a problem with food. Don't blame food for the state of your body. You must love food, enjoy cooking and eating – just get to know the difference between what's healthy and what's not.

Why Do You Eat the Way You Do?

When I was about 13 years old I remember running home and trying to sneak into the kitchen when my grandmother wasn't there to make myself something to eat before dinner. We weren't allowed in the kitchen in between meals, but when I could get away with it I'd make myself a sandwich. I'd have thick white bread, buttered, and I'd cover it in tomato ketchup. It was gorgeous, so good – and so bad for me. No wonder my grandmother didn't want us snacking in between meals.

I think food is very much attached to memories and that often we stick to certain foods because they remind us of something. We have an emotional attachment and we want to keep repeating the memory a particular food conjures up but, as we get older, our bodies change and we can't keep eating the same foods. Can you imagine how big I'd be if I was still making those ketchup sandwiches?

When I was 18 I loved ham and cheese deep-pan pizza. That's what I'd eat maybe four/five times a week. Now I just think – *lard!* I was so skinny then,

I could get away with eating stuff like that, but no way could I now, and I wouldn't even want to because I'm aware of what I eat. These days pizza, full of salt, fat and starch – just the kind of food to make me bloated – is off the menu.

I was able to eat rice and fish 10 years ago, but I can't anymore. Now I know that not mixing protein and carbs works with my body so I go with it. I can have the fish, but not with the rice, and if I want the rice I can't have the fish. If I fancy a roast dinner I have one, but I don't have the roast potatoes and Yorkshire pudding.

We all have to evolve when it comes to what we eat and find out what's right for us. It doesn't mean giving yourself a hard time or going hungry. It just means eating good, healthy food 90 per cent of the time and having treats 10 per cent of the time. It's when it's the other way round you're in trouble.

A lot of people continue eating the way they always have as they get older and their bodies don't like it. You may have been able to eat lots of salt, sugar and fat when you were younger, but you can't do it when you get older. You actually need to eat less, so adjusting how much you eat as well as what you eat makes a big difference. And yes, you might be a bit bigger than you used to be because that tends to happen anyway, but you can still be lean, firm and fit.

Forget about the memory a particular food once held for you and instead think about whether it's still right for you now. Think before you eat. When you feel like eating a whole bar of chocolate the size of a brick ask yourself *why*. Is it because you really want the chocolate or is it more to do with being stressed/unhappy/depressed/bored? It really pays to stop and think.

There's nothing worse than eating something and afterwards thinking, 'I wish I hadn't done that.' You don't want to feel bloated and bad and guilty. It's much nicer to sit back and say, 'Yeah, that was nice, I feel good now.'

Be the Right Size for You

Back in the days when I was busy starving myself to death, crash-dieting so I'd look thin on my album covers, the more weight I lost the better everyone told me I looked. I was really thin, which was all that mattered in the music industry. Now, though, when I look back at some of those old pictures I think I actually look a bit hard and bony. There's something cold and androgynous that I don't like.

The woman looking back at me comes across as unapproachable and tough, not warm and loveable. She's not the kind of woman you'd want to hug and she's so thin that if you did she'd be all bones and sharp angles, not soft and feminine. *I* don't even want to hug me looking like that. I think that when you're obsessed with being thin, you sacrifice your femininity.

I went to Jamaica when I was skinny and everyone there told me to eat some food, whereas in London they all thought I looked fantastic. See the difference? Now I'm bigger I love the way I look, love my curves – and I love the fact I can express my softer side.

Right now there's a huge obsession with being extremely thin. Everyone's talking about size 0, which is about the size of a healthy seven-year-old. Why would any normal woman aspire to that? And why are we so caught up with admiring women with no bodies? I don't get it. Whatever happened to admiring women with brains?

I admire women like Oprah, Queen Latifah, Barbra Streisand, who don't have bodies like supermodels but happen to be great women anyway.

I don't admire women who are photographed all the time and splashed across every magazine and newspaper just for being thin. I wonder what these women, so-called style icons, are actually *doing*. They're wealthy and powerful, always in the public eye, always shopping, but not actually doing anything. Their lives are based on vanity.

Real women are out working, looking after children, running a home, and all the rest. I know who I consider is making a bigger contribution.

It's time we shifted our way of thinking because we're looking up to the wrong women. We need to learn to admire great women, not great waistlines.

I don't care what anyone says about what's fashionable or not, I don't believe being skinny is healthy. It can't be. If you're yo-yo dieting and your weight's going up and down, you're probably damaging your immune system. What happens when you get sick and your body's natural defence system is so weak it can't fight back?

> We need to learn to admire great women, not great waistlines

Size 0 women really don't look well. They look like they're suffering from malnutrition and they're definitely storing up problems for later. Once they get older and their bones start crumbling, they'll snap. Brittle bone disease – osteoporosis – is a massive problem for women and crash dieting doesn't help. Diets are short-term solutions in return for long-term pain. I don't know about you, but I want to be well because health is wealth.

Calcium

I swear by calcium. If I don't have enough in my diet, I can feel the difference. I used to suffer really bad neck and shoulder pain after a car accident. As soon as I started taking calcium supplements, it went. Although the experts say there is no proof, I'm sure it helps the pain for me. Women need calcium. It's essential for strong bones and teeth and to keep muscles and nerves healthy. It's calming, it helps keep your skin looking good. What's not to like about it?

If you don't get enough calcium in your diet, you're going to be more prone to osteoporosis and when your bones are thinner there's more chance of breaks and fractures. Around 1 in 12 women over the age of 50 suffers from osteoporosis and some experts think low calcium intake among young women, which may have something to do with the trend for dairy-free diets,

means we're on course for an epidemic of
brittle bone disease in the future. If you're
not eating dairy, you need to get your
calcium from another source, or take a daily
supplement. I take 2000mg of calcium a
day and I couldn't do without it.

> # Health is wealth

You should have at least 700mg of calcium, about a pint of milk, a day.
If you're having milk on cereal and in hot drinks, it soon adds up to what
your body needs. Eating plenty of yoghurt daily will also do the trick. You
can also get calcium from leafy green vegetables like kale, spinach, broccoli
and watercress. Sesame seeds are another good source. It's worth bearing in
mind, though, that milk is the cheap and easy way to get your calcium. You'd
have to eat sixteen portions of spinach to get as much calcium as a single glass
of milk provides.

Research has shown that calcium has a role to play in weight loss.
A study in the US found that it may aid weight loss in overweight
individuals. Women in their fifties who took 500mg of calcium
supplements daily gained 1.8 kilograms less over a 10-year period than
women who weren't on supplements.

Starflower Oil

I found out a few years back that my hormones were out of whack and it was
making me moody and miserable. Around my period I'd get so stressed, have
these awful depressions and just feel erratic. I think a lot of women suffer
with their hormones, find themselves losing it and going a bit crazy around
the time of the month, and think, 'It's me – I'm just a moody cow.' Chances
are you've got some kind of hormonal imbalance.

I discovered Starflower oil, which is a great source of Gamma Linolenic
Acid, containing twice the level found in Evening Primrose Oil. It's brilliant.
I take a supplement called Floresse, which I get from Boot's. It's a really

concentrated dose – 1000mg – and I take it every day for two weeks before my period. I'm sure it chills me out, calms me down, and stops me lashing out. If I get period pains, backache, anything like that, I'm convinced that Starflower oil knocks it on the head. It seems to work for me. It's great for your skin, too.

Another great supplement is Brewer's Yeast. I took it for morning sickness when I was pregnant and it did the trick, but it also makes your skin look amazing. It's a good source of protein and one of the best sources of B vitamins there is. Brewer's Yeast contains 17 vitamins – including B6, thiamine, riboflavin, niacin, biotin and folic acid – and all the essential amino acids. It's packed with 14 minerals – including zinc, iron, phosphorous and selenium.

Greens

It's always best to get nutrients from a healthy and balanced diet and supplements cannot replace that, but I've found that certain supplements really give me a boost.

I used to take Spirulina, which contains loads of nutrients and antioxidants: beta-carotene, Vitamin B12, iron, trace minerals, gamma-linolenic acid, and chlorophyll, the pigment that makes plants green. Then, on a trip to Australia, someone told me about liquid chlorophyll, and now I take that, just add it to my bottled water every day, and it's fantastic. It's made from alfalfa and it's purifying, cleanses the blood, and helps the body flush out toxins. I feel more energised and I rarely get sick now. About the worst I'll get is a cold that's gone in a day or two.

Some people believe that we need to get the acid/alkaline balance in our diets right and green supplements can help. Apparently, our diet should be around 80 per cent alkaline and 20 per cent acid, but most of us eat too many acid-forming foods.

Red meat, coffee, alcohol, hard cheese, bread and sugar are all acid-forming. Stress is also a factor because it makes the body more acidic.

Lemons, alfalfa, mangoes, apples, watercress, and green vegetables like broccoli and spinach, are good alkalisers.

Work with What You Have

I think we have to make our health a priority and stop wanting to be something we're not. I want women to make the best of what they have, feel confident in their skin. If you're excessively overweight I'll give you a hard time, but the fact is we come in different shapes and sizes. You can just as easily be a fit and shapely size 14 as a 10.

I don't have the perfect body according to all the magazines, but I do have the perfect body for me. I can do any photo shoot, get my make-up girl, and a stylist, order dresses in a size 14 – and a 16 because some are going to come up small – and I guarantee I'll look so hot you won't even be thinking about my size.

I don't think size 14 is big, it's normal to me, but sometimes I'll ask to borrow a dress for a shoot and the company will turn round and say they don't do size 14. They can kiss my arse. I'm not going to let that make me feel insecure about my size. If being a size 14 is seen as fat, then we're really screwed.

We all know how we like to look, what makes us feel good, and that's what counts. I put it like this: as long as I take my clothes off and can stand in front of the mirror in my bra and knickers and see that my body is in proportion, that's what I like. It's not about being Giselle or Sophie Anderton, it's not about any of those people – it's about being *you*.

When I look at my body and I see I'm a good shape, nice and firm, I'm happy. I'm happy I can show off my tummy even though I only had a baby last year. I don't need a washboard stomach and I don't need to be Naomi Campbell. It wouldn't make me happier because I love what I am, I work on what I have, and when you do that you start to fall in love with yourself and feel satisfied.

If you look in the mirror and you've got stuff hanging off, skin folding where it shouldn't, then it's a sign you need to make some changes. No one wants to look at themselves and hate what they see, so just be aware of what you're eating, cut out the bad stuff, and two months down the line I guarantee you'll feel wicked.

I'm not a model, so I don't need to look like one. That's someone else's job. I think the images we're fed are really damaging and the trouble is women are looking at magazines, comparing themselves, and making themselves feel crap because they're *normal*, not a size 0. Stop it. Just because you look at pictures of those skinny girls doesn't mean you have to be them. Just remember, those girls are doing a job. Being a model is their job. It's not my job and it's not yours. Do you think those models could do what I do, or what you do? No way.

We have to stop thinking that being skin and bone is the only thing that matters. I've met lots of models and they always look unhappy and insecure. They look just like I did when I wasn't eating. I was talking to one of these girls recently and she said she wished she could be like me and not care. Actually, I do care. I'm not a slob, I look after myself, but I'm not going to starve myself to look a certain way. I've tried it and it doesn't work. There's something quite depreciating about being a model. Basically, they're clothes hangers and these stick-thin girls end up feeling as if they have no worth.

The irony is so many women spend their time looking at pictures of models wishing they could be just like that, when in fact the girls they are aspiring to be are utterly miserable.

Are You Ready for Change?

I work out three times a week, if I can. I might go to the gym, do 20 minutes on the cross-trainer, some crunches, 10 minutes on the treadmill, work up a sweat, and that's it. Exercising for around 45 minutes three times a week keeps me feeling good. We all need to exercise, find something that suits us, and let off steam. The body likes to move. When you're not doing anything physical, you pay the price.

Regular exercise is good for all kinds of reasons.

- It makes you look better.
- It helps balance your blood-sugar levels.
- It helps reduce cravings and gives you more energy.
- It boosts your metabolism.
- It releases endorphins that make you feel good, give you a buzz, keep you calm, and help you concentrate.

Maybe you think you don't have time to exercise, but you have to make time to be disciplined and put the work in. Go for three 10-minute walks a day if that's easier than finding half an hour to spare. If you really want to change, you'll find the time. It's easy to make excuses, but all that happens is you end up stuck in a rut, feeling miserable and fed up because nothing is changing.

When I see someone who is overweight to the point where nothing fits, and they're heading for obesity, I know they're not happy with their lives, that something is hurting. Comfort eating and sitting with the remote in your hand watching TV isn't going to help.

Would you rather have a nagging voice in your head making you feel bad about yourself? Do you really want to be thinking, 'God, I feel fat today'?

That voice stops when you start training and putting in the time to work out. It shuts up. But when you're not doing anything, not working on your body, you're in a negative place, constantly thinking you're rubbish and feeling fat all the time.

I know just how that feels. In your heart you know you should be training and the guilt of doing nothing just makes you feel worse and worse. It doesn't help to put it off and think, 'Oh I'll just go down the crash diet road for a few weeks, that'll make me feel better.' It won't. That's only going to makes you feel worse, hungry, deprived, irritable, and craving all the stuff you're not allowed to eat.

Stick to good food, make exercise part of your life and you'll feel and look better. When you're conscious about your health and ready to make some positive changes, you'll find that leads you to take action.

Positive thinking and a willingness to change makes you want to get busy and *do* something. And when you start with getting active and eating healthy food it has a positive effect on how you *think*. It's a two-way process. One complements the other.

I've got a friend who's struggling with her weight, going to the gym, working out, and not seeing results because she still has bad habits with food. She's eating too many carbs – white bread, pasta, rice, you name it – and she's not eating enough protein.

The girl is drop dead gorgeous, but her weight is really getting her down. She put on a stone recently and can't shift it, even though she's training. All I want to know is whether she's ready to change the way she eats, but she reckons if she doesn't load up on carbs she starts to feel light-headed.

You don't get light-headed when you're eating well, when you're sitting down to a nice big piece of roast chicken and a huge portion of broccoli. You get light-headed when you're not eating enough and your body's not getting enough nutrients. And you get light-headed when you're dehydrated, so make sure you're drinking plenty of water. Put a slice of lemon in it if you like, just try to get 1–2 litres every day to stay hydrated and flush out toxins.

What I say to my friend is that working out isn't enough *on its own*. Eating good food isn't enough *on its own*. The two go hand in hand and if you don't have the right balance you'll struggle to see results. Don't tell yourself you can keep on eating rubbish because you go to the gym – you can't. It's cheating the body and it doesn't work. You have to break bad eating habits and replace them with good ones, however much exercise you are doing.

Do What Suits You

I know that some women don't like the idea of going to the gym. If your confidence is on the floor sometimes the last thing you feel like doing is going to a gym where it's unfamiliar and there are people who are fitter and slimmer than you. If you feel this way, go to the park instead of the gym and jog or walk. Walking is so good for you. Do half an hour a day and you'll be amazed at the difference it makes. You'll tone up your legs and your stomach. Any time your stomach feels big it's because you're not using your legs, so get out there and walk, walk, walk. Make it a habit. Give it two months and I promise you'll be looking better, feeling stronger, be more energised. There's something about exercising outside that feels really good. It clears your head and gets you thinking straight, as well as getting you fitter. When I run in the park, I feel different inside and it shows on the outside.

Once you start training you have to keep pushing your body, keep giving it a shock, making it work harder. A lot of the time people go to the gym and do the same exercise day in, day out. They get on the cross-trainer and keep the gauge at the same level or the treadmill at the same speed because that's their comfort zone. It's not going to work. The body needs resistance, that's what it likes, and that's when it's going to burn energy. You see people in the gym and they're not even breaking a sweat and you're like, 'What the hell did you do?'

Gradually increase the intensity of the exercise. Get on the cross-trainer and go to the next level, keep the gauge going up. Don't just stick to the programme you know. Try a different one. Don't let your body get used to it – keep shocking it with new stuff.

If you want to get lean, you need to do aerobic exercise: walking, running, using the cross-trainer, swimming. Join a class, work up a sweat. Leave out the weights until you've stripped the fat then, if you want that defined look, like Madonna, do some resistance work.

A Change for Life

I look at my friend and I know I could have her looking banging in four months, but she's stubborn, not willing to give up the bad food yet, and that's what's holding her back. What I'm recommending isn't the easy option. It's not a 30-day programme. It's a lifestyle change and it's for serious women, women who are willing to work. It's not about short-lived instant gratification. I remember the days when I'd get by on coffee and smoke to take the edge off my appetite, and, yeah, the weight fell off, but I felt rubbish.

Lots of us count on that caffeine high to keep us going when there's no food in our system, but endless cups of coffee will dehydrate you and after the high comes the crash, when you realise you're starving and you tear into all the stuff you're trying not to eat that's full of sugar and fat. Then afterwards you feel bad. Starving and bingeing is a vicious cycle.

Get some balance in your diet and you won't need all that coffee to keep going. Decide you only want to eat good food and you'll find it's only once in a while you want that Krispy Kreme doughnut or that bag of chips, and because you know your body is being trained every week, from time to time you can have those treats and not feel guilty. It's about balance in everything.

Never Write People Off

I was in the gym recently and a girl I didn't know, just someone I'd seen around, came up to me. 'I can't believe you're the same person,' she said. 'I remember seeing you a while back and you were so big I was thinking why do you even bother coming to the gym?'

I said, 'Well, it just goes to show, you should never write anyone off.'

I probably hadn't seen this girl for around 14 months and, to be honest, I wasn't that big then, maybe a stone heavier than I am now. I was also pregnant.

She kept looking at me and saying, 'Your face looks so long now – what have you done?' I told her I hadn't done anything apart from lose weight, but I could see she didn't believe me, couldn't understand that the reason I'm looking better is because my life's in balance, and that's down to a simple routine of eating well, being active, and drinking lots of water.

It was obvious she thought I'd had some work done, been off and had plastic surgery, but I would never touch my face.

You don't need plastic surgery when you're looking after yourself because it takes years off you anyway. That's one of the biggest changes I've seen. Health and vitality gives you a glow from inside.

What I've Learned

- Focus on healthy eating, not being skinny
- Be conscious of what you are putting into your body – aim to eat healthily 90 per cent of the time
- Drink two litres of water daily
- Health supplements can make a difference
- Take regular moderate exercise

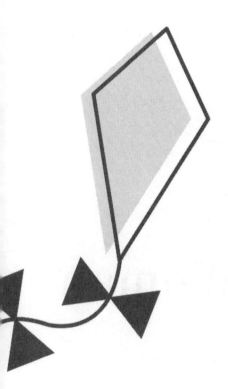

Warrior Woman

Three weeks after giving birth to Russia I was working, breastfeeding in the morning and again at night, doing 13–14-hour days presenting the TV series *What Not To Wear*.

There were times I was so tired my eyes were burning, but I was glad to work, to have the distraction, to be doing something that helped other women. I really needed it.

What I'd been through with Andreas was heart-wrenching. I was crying every day, in so much pain. It was work that helped me start to heal.

I'd landed the show when I was six months pregnant, not knowing then just how much I was going to need it. I don't think it was a fluke it came along when it did; it was definitely meant to be.

Doing a full-on, full-time job probably isn't what most women would choose straight after having a baby, but it was the best thing for me. I was working with women every day who had their own problems and that took my mind off mine.

I couldn't spend hours going over what had gone wrong because I didn't have the time and by the time we finished filming the series, five months later, I wasn't hurting as much. I thought, 'There are worse things in life.' It really doesn't pay to re-play pain.

My grandmother has the right attitude. She says, 'Just get on with your life, keep praying, and focus on doing great work. That's all you do. Don't worry about any of the other stuff, just focus on your work. Put your head there and everything will come back to you, everything you want – everything you don't even know you want. It will all be yours.'

And she's absolutely right.

Having it All

My grandmother is a real inspiration to me. She came to England from Jamaica, no idea what she was letting herself in for, what she'd find, just an absolute determination to succeed. She started from scratch, found work, put in the hours, and saved up to bring my grandad and the children over. She had four or five jobs at a time, and she just grafted non-stop. She had her goal in sight and she wasn't going to let anything get in the way.

She's a doer and she just kept going, pushing herself, doing great things. In the end, she didn't just save enough to bring her family over, she managed to do something pretty amazing and buy a three-storey Victorian house in Lewisham. My grandmother is a real warrior woman.

As a kid I saw her doing all her different jobs, running a home, bringing up a family, never letting anything limit her or hold her back. She was confident, always looked good – just bloody remarkable. Nothing stopped her. She'd come down the road with seven or eight bags of groceries, cook for everyone, go to church, go out and have fun, never complain. I wanted to be just like her, have the strong marriage, the family, the relationship with God, all kinds of great stuff going on.

She showed me that you can have it all, that you can be a mother and still have a loving relationship, and a career – lots of different careers, in fact – and still have fun. The only thing stopping you is yourself.

I feel blessed to have had my grandmother as a role model when I was growing up. She was a great example of what you can achieve through sheer hard work and perseverance. She knew what was important, knew her own worth, and that's what I want. It's not about being Superwoman, it's about doing all the things you're passionate about because that's what you enjoy.

I think women are amazing, that every one of us is capable of doing great things, but that, mostly, we're only fulfilling a fraction of our potential. We've somehow got side-tracked about what's really important. An awful lot of women today are obsessed only with being stick thin, having perfect nails, doing whatever it takes to stay looking young. In today's society it's more about what's on the surface that counts, not what's going on inside and, increasingly, that's how women are judged. The ones that come closest to the so-called physical ideal are deemed desirable and successful, and the ones that don't are written off as inferior, as failures. It's appalling.

Age is No Obstacle

Everybody is so afraid of getting old these days. There's a huge obsession with staying young-looking – at any cost. Cosmetic surgery is a massive multi-million pound industry and it's no longer only for the rich and famous. Women from all walks of life are prepared to spend huge amounts of money on operations they think are going to make them look and feel better: a face lift, a nose job, new cheekbones, fake breasts, whatever it might be.

They compare themselves to the celebrities in magazines – women who always manage to look 'perfect', seem to have the whole business of ageing under control – and feel second rate. Let's not forget that many of those images are airbrushed by the magazines as well. Some women even ask surgeons to make them look like their favourite celebrity because they're don't like who they are. How sick is that?

When you go down that road what you're actually saying is you don't believe you're good enough. You don't feel special or unique the way you are.

You don't value yourself. Wanting to look like someone else says you have no self-worth, no sense of your unique value.

You convince yourself the celebrity you're obsessed with has the life you want and that, if only you looked more like her, your life would be better. You tell yourself that's why you're not successful, why you can't meet anyone. You feel like Billy No Mates, and believe that if you change your face everything else is going to change, too. That a nip and a tuck is going to make all the difference. A bit of surgery and you'll suddenly feel loved. New face, new life.

So, you go for it, the doctor cuts up your face, does exactly what you want, and when you come out you realise nothing's changed. You *still* feel like Billy No Mates, only now you've got a new nose and different cheekbones.

This whole obsession with surgery is so destructive. I don't believe women need plastic surgery. I don't believe they need to have stuff injected into their skin to freeze lines or to make their lips look fuller. To me, it's toxic and it's never-ending. You're just going to keep going back for more. I've seen really pretty girls who've ruined their looks by going under the knife. They go for more and more extreme results until they look hideous. Jocelyn Wildenstein, who has had a lot of surgery, is the perfect example of everything that's wrong with our society.

I don't see why we're so frightened of getting old. I feel better now than I did 10 years ago. I look better, too. I don't think looking good, holding back time, is about having surgery. It's more to do with how you feel inside.

I don't dwell on getting older or obsess about getting lines. I just don't think about it. I'm more interested in living, engaging in things that stimulate my mind. It all comes back to fulfilling your potential.

> I don't dwell on getting older. I'm more interested in living

When that's what you're doing you haven't got time to think about getting old. People make the mistake of thinking *old* means *over*. It doesn't. I've seen people thinking themselves into old age, making the ageing process an obsession. They believe everything stops when they reach a certain point, that all kinds of things are off-limits, so they give up. It doesn't have to be like that. Age doesn't have to be an obstacle.

Eternal Youth

Positive thinking plays a major part in how you feel and look. If you make up your mind to slow down, take things easy, you're telling your body you don't expect great things of it anymore, and if that's what the body is hearing, day in, day out, it's going to absorb that message and start easing up. If you really live your life to the full, though, keep chasing your dreams and doing the things you're passionate about, you're sending out a much more positive signal.

What's stopping you? So often people are held back by that old enemy fear: fear of the unknown, fear of failing, fear of what other people might think. If we let it, fear can stop us in our tracks. We limit ourselves because we're scared, and the older we get the more afraid we become.

Failure doesn't seem so bad when you're young. We just get up and have another go. The whole point about life, though, is it's a journey into the unknown and that means taking chances, messing up, getting it wrong sometimes. All those things are just part of the process. Getting older doesn't mean having to put the brakes on. It doesn't mean choosing the safe option every time. Sometimes we need to give ourselves a fright, come out of our comfort zone. We need a kick up the backside now and then because, without it, we become more fearful and we start to stagnate. We have to keep looking at life as an adventure, a rollercoaster – something exhilarating. That way you're so busy having the time of your life that getting older becomes secondary. It's not the big obsession anymore.

There are people in their eighties and nineties out there still doing great things: running marathons, studying, teaching, travelling the world, doing voluntary work, writing, painting, performing, you name it. You don't have to stop. I look at life as a series of challenges from start to finish. You don't just master one thing and then sit back – you're always looking for the next challenge, wondering what else you can do, how much further you can go. And, if you can do that as you get older, that's a major achievement.

What really counts is your relationship with yourself, your state of mind. What so many people don't realise is *that's* the key to prolonging life, the secret of eternal youth. Everyone is searching for a magic pill or potion, but we already have it – it's inside every single one of us.

My family couldn't care less about age. My mum looks like she could be my sister. My grandmother is in her eighties, but looks like she could be my mum. Some of it's down to genes, but mostly it's about how they feel about themselves and life.

Having an optimistic outlook is a key ingredient to staying young-looking. If you feel good about life, channel your thoughts into achieving great things, and believe your purpose is to fulfil your destiny, it's written all over your face. The way you feel inside is *always* reflected on the outside.

When people talk about worrying themselves sick they're not kidding. Being anxious about ageing and wrinkles, writing yourself off with every passing year, *will* make you old. Plastic surgery is not the answer. It's just another addiction, another quick-fix.

Where does it end? You have the facelift, then you start hating your nose.

A few years on and you start seeing a few more lines so you decide you need another facelift. And so it goes on. One day you look in the mirror and you don't even look like you anymore. You have that strange, tight, unnatural 'done' look, and there's no going back.

Bag a Rich Guy?

Lots of women today believe their purpose in life is to bag a rich guy and let him take care of them. That's their dream, their sole ambition.

They're not thinking about what great things they might achieve or what they might have to contribute to the planet. They're counting on a wealthy guy to come along and pick up the tab forever, and all they need to do in return is look beautiful. I know a lot of women who think there's nothing wrong with that, that living off a man is fine, but I have a real issue with it.

I actually think there's nothing more sexy than meeting someone who has their own, someone self-sufficient who is doing great things with their life. Those people have a confidence and an energy that's incredibly attractive. They're in control of their own destiny and it shows. It sets them apart, gives them an extra-special something that everyone else picks up on.

They're life's doers, the ones who get up and get out there and make things happen. They're not sitting back waiting for someone else to do the work. That's such a powerful thing and it doesn't just apply to men. The same goes for women.

The woman who follows her passion, achieves success on her own terms, and grabs life with both hands, has so much more going for her than the one who sits back, expecting a man to keep her. Who would you rather be?

I think too many women under-value themselves. They're not thinking about what they can achieve in their own right, what they can bring to a relationship. They're thinking about finding someone who can give them the lifestyle they want. Get the rich guy and live happy ever after.

That's not how it works, though. Co-dependent relationships are destructive. I'm testament to that. When the man you're with has all the money, he also has the power and, in the long-term, that does nothing for your sense of self-worth. A strong, self-sufficient man is going to want to be with a woman who is also that way. That's what he admires.

Relationships can't be all about looks. The woman who looks fantastic but has nothing going on inside, isn't going to hold the interest of a successful, high-achieving man. He'll get bored fast. We all want to look good, but beauty is skin deep. On its own it's too shallow and superficial to engage someone's interest. I'm not saying you won't get the guy. I know girls who've married millionaires. The trick, though, is keeping them.

Is a successful, wealthy man really going to be content with a woman who does nothing more than shop and have her nails done? Surely that would bore him in 10 seconds flat. If all he wants is a good-looking girl on his arm, what's to stop him swapping you for someone else? There are loads of pretty girls out there.

Alpha Females

I think women have to take stock, reassess the way they view themselves.

We have to constantly remind ourselves that we have our own aspirations and goals and focus on them. Be an alpha female, have a sense of purpose, chase your dreams regardless of whether there's a man in your life or not.

Make it about *you*.

These days, too many women are looking to sit in the passenger seat of the Ferrari, like some kind of optional extra. Come *on*. If that's all you are, you can be replaced at any time. Any other beautiful girl can sit in that passenger seat and it's not going to make the slightest bit of difference.

I don't know about you, but I don't just want to be in the passenger seat – I want to know that I own half the car.

When you're both contributing, you're not taxing the relationship. You're not going to have those feelings of frustration further down the road. But if all you're doing is spending someone else's money, it's never going to last. It doesn't matter how wealthy a guy is, he's going to get sick of the fact that you're taking and taking all the time.

He's going to start to wonder whether it's him you love or the lifestyle he provides, and that's when he's going to start resenting you. That's when his self-esteem starts getting whacked as well. He will definitely get tired of you if all you're doing is getting your hair done, going for Botox, shopping every day – and he's paying for it all. It doesn't pay in the end because all you're doing is making yourself disposable. He sees those chicks every day, the ones with the perfect nails and hair, the whole package, and he can take his pick.

You have to think about what you have that makes you special because that's the difference between a short-term, throw-away relationship and one that lasts.

I know very successful and wealthy young men who are starting to get really tired of superficial women. They find them too frivolous. You have to remember that when a man has done really well and he's at the top of his game, he's the king. What he's looking for is a queen, not a maid pretending to be a queen. He can find that anywhere. What's attractive to him is a woman who is as focused as he is on getting her life together, who has a plan, a talent, a career, something tangible to offer. Looks aren't everything. They're only a part of what you are. What's more important is being able to engage with someone mentally. It's the most attractive thing in the world.

A lot of women see their role in life as finding the wealthy husband, having the fairytale wedding, living the pampered, privileged life, never having to lift a finger. Think how bored you're going to get. Think how bored *he's* going to get. We have to kill the whole fairytale thing and get real, do the work on ourselves, and that way we'll get the life we want. You can have the man and the wealthy lifestyle. You can have it all, but it starts with you.

Know Your Purpose

Living the life you want always starts with finding the thing you're passionate about – whatever it is you love doing – and making that your career. Being paid for doing the thing you love gives you confidence and boosts your self-esteem. Knowing you can make money from whatever gift you have sets you apart, changes your whole outlook, gives you freedom. You're not living some soulless existence doing a job you hate, wishing some guy would come along and whisk you away. You're at peace with yourself because *you're* creating the life you want. You don't need someone else to do it for you.

You're not obsessed with getting the rich guy in the expensive car because you don't need him. Once you find your purpose in life and *act on it,* it's amazing how you change your view. The guy in the Porsche might well come along and if he does, great, but you're not looking to him to rescue you. You're not looking to him to provide for you because you're already providing for yourself.

The woman who thinks the rich guy is the answer to her prayers is waiting for him to fill the void in her life, but that's not how it works.

You have to fill the void yourself.

I don't look at relationships in terms of what I can get out of them. If you're doing that, you're coming from a cynical place. I'm just looking for someone to hang out with, someone it's great to be around. When attraction is about status or power or fame or money, or any of that stuff, it has no real substance. Love gets lost somewhere along the way.

I don't believe opportunism can ever be a good foundation for a loving relationship. If you're with someone because of the lifestyle they can give you or the doors they can open, and all you're doing is feeding off them, it's not love. A productive partnership is one where there's give and take, where you help each other grow and develop.

People aren't there to be used and tossed aside. There has to be integrity on both sides. If one person is sucking the life out of the other, how can that ever be fulfilling? You only have to look at a person to know if what they have with the other person is edifying. Relationships need balance. They're a two-way thing.

When two strong, independent souls come together there's no insecurity on either side because you're both content with where you're at in life, and you're not looking to the other person to make you whole.

I look at my grandparents, both of them were working, bringing in money, each one was contributing. First and foremost they were powerful individuals and, together, they made an awesome team. What they had was built on granite, not sand.

Women who pin everything on a rich dude are basically saying they have no sense of self-worth and no means of self-fulfilment. They dream of the guy coming along on the white horse and taking them off the council estate, but they're missing the point. They already have it within themselves to make their dreams come true. We all do.

What Do Women Want?

I think low self-esteem is less of a problem among black women and I'm not sure why that is; perhaps it's because in black culture women are celebrated and seen as the backbone of family life. All the women in my family are strong, confident characters. We're close, too, almost like a sisterhood, and perhaps you don't find that so much in white families.

In black families the men are off watching the cricket, or whatever, and the women hang out together, cook together, and look out for each other. We tell each other we look good and, if someone's down, the rest of us pull them back up. That's how all women have to be.

There is a big difference between being obsessed with your looks – having surgery etc. – and taking pride in your appearance. The way I was brought up, it was a big thing to look your best, to do the family proud when you went out. Everyone in my family made an effort to look good all the time. If you looked decent, people treated you with respect. My parents were always decked out in really stylish, designer clothes. My grandparents were more conservative, but never failed to look neat and tidy. My grandad wore a tie every day of his life. No one would have dreamed of letting themselves go. We all understood that looking good made us feel good. That whole thing of looking your best at all times is something I still do now.

We have to keep reminding ourselves we're on this planet to fulfil our potential and make that the starting point. It's about waking up and taking a long, hard look at what we're really doing – being conscious. You can't go through life on auto-pilot, disconnected, asleep.

Ask yourself if you're happy with the way things are and think hard about what it is you need to change. Get to know the *real* you, the person behind the mask, find out what makes you tick, what motivates and stimulates you.

Work on yourself.

- Are you nourishing your body with good food?
- Are you doing regular exercise?
- Are you in a job you hate – or doing the thing you're passionate about?

What I'm advocating is a way of life and it's not easy. I struggle with stuff every day. Being self-aware, changing your life, takes work. Every day I wake up and have to *consciously* remember I have work to do. I have to make that conscious effort and I always know when I haven't because I get that self-loathing thing kicking in. And whenever I start to feel like that, I know I have some serious work to do.

Be Consistent

We're in the age of the short attention span. A lot of people don't have the patience to follow things through. They start something, lose interest when it gets a bit tough, and don't see it through to the end, but it's consistency that brings success. Persevering is what brings results, and that's what we have to teach our kids.

I say never give up, no matter how bad things look. I don't care if you tell me a million times I can't do something, I'm so stubborn I'm gonna keep going, and that's how we all have to be. I'm not saying it's easy or that you won't fall on your face a few times, but you have to get up again and keep at it, even when it feels like all the odds are stacked against you.

You can't let setbacks stand in your way. You have to overcome them. When I had record companies telling me I'm a has-been I just thought, 'Yeah, okay, I'm a has-been to you but I'm not a has-been to me. I can still get up and have another go.'

Even when something has knocked me flat and I've ended up depressed, broke, no idea what I'm going to do next, I still somehow find a way to try again. It comes back to having faith and holding onto your self-belief, even when no one else believes in you.

Self-belief is not about arrogance. It's about strength and determination, having confidence, trusting you're on the right path even when it doesn't look like it.

I was brought up to believe I could do anything if I put my mind to it. My grandparents let me know the value and meaning of life, of being selfless, treating people well, having respect. I grew up with a sense of consciousness, knowing right from wrong. My grandmother taught me to be humble, always keep my feet on the ground, be grateful, never bite the hand that feeds. It was a very old-fashioned upbringing, very strict and disciplined,

Self-belief is not about arrogance. It's about strength and determination

but it gave me moral fibre. We had boundaries and overstepping the mark was just not tolerated.

When I was about 11 years old I went to the local corner shop, picked up a packet of crisps, and took them without paying. I was so pleased with myself. When I got home my grandmother was furious. She said, 'Take them back *now*.' How many mothers would turn a blind eye? I've seen kids nicking stuff and parents doing nothing about it. 'Oh, it's only a packet of crisps.' It's not, though – it's about knowing it's wrong to steal. Full stop. We need to be on our kids all the time so they know when they do wrong. I'm so grateful to my grandparents. They knew the difference and they made sure we did, too. Old is gold, as far as I'm concerned.

Old is gold

Be a Conscious Parent

I believe in being a conscious parent. Conscious parenting means you set the trend, you set the pace, and your children follow because they learn about life in the home. I heard someone talking about footballers and celebrities being role models for our children, but I just don't get that. *We* have to be the role models for our kids. They copy everything we do, good and bad.

If you're honest, your kids will be honest. If you're stand-offish, they will be stand-offish. If you're cold, they will be, too. If you're loving, they'll do the same. We're all a product of our parenting. That's why most of us have to go back and repair the damage when we're older; because whatever problems we have go back to what we experienced when we were little.

No one can tell me that a child is born naughty and that's the end of it. The child always learns their behaviour from the parent. If my daughter gets a bad report, it's my fault. I don't look for someone else to blame – her father, my mother, the school, the next-door neighbour – *I* take responsibility.

I know that everything I do rubs off on my children. No one gives you a manual on parenting, though; you just have to feel your way. I knew how I wanted to bring up my children because of the way I was brought up. My grandparents were very moral and principled. They taught us to value and respect each other, to be selfless, to be giving, not to just think about ourselves. What I got from them was a sense of empathy for other people and I think that's really important. The people who cause the most hurt are always the selfish ones, the ones who have no empathy. When you bring up your children to be sensitive to the needs of others, you're teaching them the value of making people happy – *and* the positive knock-on effect of that for themselves. If the people around them are happy, they're happy. If that's how you think, that's how they'll think, but if you're only thinking about your own needs and wants, that's how your kids are going to be.

Those are the kids that end up out there hurting other people because that's what they've learned at home.

Laying Down the Law

It pays to be honest with your kids, and it also pays to let them know you're not always going to get it right. What you're creating is a relationship where there's respect, where the parent is the one to say what goes. There has to be a line kids know they can't cross.

I'm not saying you can't learn from them and I'm not saying they can't question you either. My daughter knows she can ask me anything, but she also knows she can't disrespect me. That way she knows that, ultimately, it's what I say – even when it's something she doesn't want to hear – that goes.

That doesn't mean she won't try it on or that she's not going to screw up. Every child out there is going to lose their way, something's going to happen and they're going to lose the plot and do some crazy stuff, but as long as you've given them a solid foundation they'll always come home. It's the foundation that counts, the values and principles they've grown up with, that will keep them coming back. So even when they go out and have a bit of a mad episode with their mates something in their conscience makes them stop and think, 'Hang on, I shouldn't be doing this.'

When you instil a belief system into a child, it never leaves them. They have to know right from wrong.

Most parents are too liberal, too afraid to chastise their children, to lay down the law, but that's what we must do. Sometimes you're going to feel like a military sergeant, but you have be that way because kids need discipline – in every area of life.

Parents can't be a walkover and kids have to know that. If you don't put them in line, they're going to start taking over and then you'll end up with no power, no authority. Be tough. Don't let them skip school once the exams are over. Make them go because that's telling them that good attendance, being conscientious, is important. Once that sinks in, that's how they'll be for the rest of their lives – reliable, consistent, following things through to the end. If you teach your children it doesn't really matter, though, that they don't need to bother, that's what filters through to every aspect of their adult lives. They'll start things, get bored, give up, never keep a job – and so on.

The same goes for food. It's up to us to make sure they have a good relationship with food. If you allow them to raid the fridge whenever they feel like it, eat what they want, have chocolate for breakfast, what's that telling them? That it's okay to eat anything anytime, to put crap in their bodies. If you know they're eating rubbish, putting on weight, getting bad skin, and you do nothing, you're not helping them.

When I was growing up if I got into trouble, my grandparents were there in a second. I'd start to say, 'But...' and they'd go *whack!* I wouldn't even get the rest of the sentence out and that discipline was what I needed to put me in line and remind me who was running things.

Traditional values just aren't there for a lot of kids today. They don't get moral fibre in their diet; they're fed materialism instead. It's all about looking bling-bling, showing off and being famous for doing jack shit. They have no consciousness and that's why we've got problems.

I'm strict with my kids because it's the only way that works, but it's a balancing act. It's about love *and* discipline.

Russia's not even a year old, but I can already see her character. I knew she was a serious chick when she started standing up at just seven months old. The girl is so determined, strong-willed, on a mission. Nothing holds her back. Those are the ones you have to watch the most, the ones that need serious discipline.

As a parent, you can't just stand back and let children have their own way. You have to keep them in line and at the same time allow them to have fun, and let them know they're loved. I think the reason we have so many problems with teenagers now is because they don't have boundaries. Kids need to know what's allowed and what isn't because that's how they learn to have respect. If you're brought up thinking anything goes, you have no control and end up hurting people. I don't think I'm being old-fashioned; it's just common sense. Boundaries work. Knowing right from wrong matters. Having respect for other people, for their space, not trying to take what isn't yours, being courteous: it all makes for a better world.

Children need to know you're the boss. No ifs or buts. They're not always going to like doing what you say, and you're not always going to get it right, but someone has to be in charge. You can't be best friends with your kids and let them do what they like. You have to be the one to lay down the law, even if they don't like you for it, otherwise they'll end up spoiled and selfish, going through life hurting people and not even knowing they're doing it.

It's not about putting a straitjacket on your kids, but it is about knowing where to draw the line because people with no boundaries *will* go out there and cause the most pain. The ones with no discipline are the most dangerous because they go through life thinking anything goes. They cause hurt and feel nothing because they have no conscience.

Women have such power. We don't just give birth, we're often the ones raising the children, and that means a huge amount of the responsibility for the next generation lies with us. We have to do our best to get it right. I don't want my daughters to grow up with no values, no respect for others, no sense of right and wrong.

I don't want them to grow up thinking they have to crash diet and starve themselves to look good. I don't want them to have eating disorders and low self-worth. I want them to be confident, to feel good about their bodies, to have a great relationship with food, to be fit and healthy.

We really have to set a good example for our kids. It all starts with us.

That's why we have to be so careful.

If what they see is us loathing our bodies, dieting, going to extremes to be thin, that's what they're going to do, too. It's up to us to raise great kids and that means watching ourselves all the time, being conscious of what we do and say. The messages they get from us must be positive. I don't believe in bringing up kids to think they're average or mediocre and that life is limiting. I believe in teaching them that life can be anything they want it to be, that they can do whatever they choose. That way we raise giants.

What I've Learned

- Ageing is nothing to be scared of – a happy life is written on your face

- Children need moral fibre, not materialism

- Finding your purpose in life is liberating – don't wait for a man to complete you

- Self-belief is about having strength and confidence

Spirit of Optimism

I've had a relationship with God for as long as I can remember.

Spirit of Optimism

When I was growing up church was an important part of my life. My grandfather was a minister and we went to church maybe six days a week. There was always something going on – Bible study, prayer meetings, choir practice or whatever. It was just something I always did and it made a big impression on me. That kind of religious upbringing made me feel I had a purpose on earth, that my existence mattered. I was taught to believe that every one of us is important. I talked to God on a daily basis, at church and at home, and that's where my faith comes from.

My faith is massive to me. I couldn't live without it. It's faith that gets me through my darkest moments, faith that gives me optimism. I think we all need to believe in something, to have some kind of spiritual connection. For me, it's at the heart of who I am.

I really believe that spirituality is bound up with everything we do and that when we work on that aspect of ourselves we make a difference in every area of life. Spirituality gives life meaning. It makes you more conscious, more selfless – more connected to the world around you.

A spiritual connection means you're never on your own, that when all else fails there's something there to hold onto, to trust and believe in. You don't even have to understand what that something is – just having a belief in a power that's bigger than you is enough.

I really believe we all need faith, that it's vital when it comes to achieving our potential, but in today's society, consumerism is the new spirituality, and a lot of people have no personal relationship with God, no sense of anything spiritual going on in their lives whatsoever.

Getting Connected

I don't go to church anymore, but I believe in the power of prayer. I take time every day to pray, to give thanks to God, and to ask for guidance. I hold regular prayer meetings at my house. Just the act of a few people getting together and asking God for good things is incredibly powerful. When you're all on the same wavelength, channelling your thoughts in the same direction, willing good things to happen, you create a powerful energy. Prayer can be the most comforting, uplifting thing.

You don't have to believe in God. You can put your faith in anything you choose – the universe, Nature, a Divine Being, a Higher Power – whatever strikes a chord. Just acknowledging that it's not all down to you, though, makes a difference to life and how you feel about it.

I think when you don't believe in anything beyond yourself and the physical world, life can be extremely tough. When it all goes bad – which it does for all of us from time to time – where do you go? Who do you turn to?

I just know that it's my faith that has kept me going through the most painful experiences, and it's faith that has given me the confidence to get back up off the floor and try again. I know the whole idea of faith and spirituality is difficult for a lot of people. Praying is second nature to me, something I've always done, but not everyone is comfortable with the idea. It takes time to develop a spiritual connection. It's not just suddenly going to be there. Like anything, when you work at it, make an effort, put in the time, you'll get there.

I actually think finding your way is as much about having the right intent as anything. When you're open and seeking answers, you're led in the direction that's right for you. Your starting point may be to seek out a pastor or a priest who can give you guidance on a spiritual level, or it may be something totally different.

Even though I grew up going to church, spirituality for me is nothing to do with religion. I actually think all religions say more or less the same thing anyway, that if you're seeking some kind of formal religious experience –

whether it's Buddhism, Christianity, Judaism or Islam – it comes down to personal choice and what feels right for you. You can only know by going there and finding out.

Spirituality is a thing that calls you and guides you when you're awake to it. Basically, once you start looking, you'll find spiritual people everywhere.

Be Open

You may not connect with the something that's right for you straight away but it's like anything new; you have to stick with it. In time, usually pretty fast, you start to find your way.

It's about being *open* to being led in a spiritual way, allowing something you can't see to guide you and trusting that your good intent will take you where you need to go – and that can be hard because deep down we're all control freaks.

Someone was talking to me about alternative therapists, saying they'd found spiritual people through things like Shiatsu and Reiki. When you have a genuine intent to be a better being, you'll find the right people to guide you and help you get there. They say that when the student is ready the teacher appears, and that's exactly how it works.

Do what feels right for you. Pay attention to your feelings and trust your instincts because that's how your spirit talks to you.

If you feel you want to see an alternative therapist, it means something in you is leading you in that direction. That's how it's meant to be. When you see that therapist, though, you must be conscious, allow yourself to *feel*, and listen to what your feelings tell you.

Focus on how you feel after the treatment. That's the important thing.

Do you feel good? Do you have a feeling of comfort? If you do, you're in the right place with the right person, but if you have to question it you know it's not right. Don't force it. We tend to be lazy and think, 'Oh, I can't be bothered to look for someone else. I'm probably just being paranoid anyway.'

No, you're not being paranoid – your spirit is telling you you're in the wrong place, so move on.

Even if the first person you go to turns out to be a charlatan, I guarantee that encounter will lead you to somebody better. If what's moving you is insincere, more about showing off than finding your spiritual path – forget it. It won't come good. If that therapy you once loved so much doesn't feel right anymore, don't worry. It's just a sign that you're growing and evolving. When you find a person you trust, tell them what you're trying to do – to connect on a spiritual level. Get into the habit of speaking to someone you trust and see what you can learn. If you don't know how to pray, ask that person, get some guidance, work it into your daily life. Set aside quiet time to ask the universe to bring great things into your life. It's going to feel weird at first, but you'll soon get the hang of it.

If you can get into the habit of taking time out each day to sit somewhere quiet, have that moment of peace and say your prayers and be sincere, you will start to notice the difference. I don't think it matters how you pray or where you go to pray. You can do it anywhere – at home, in the park, wherever feels right to you. There are no rules. Spirituality is all about your *personal relationship* with some kind of Higher Power. It can be whatever moves you. If what works for you is to light a candle in your bedroom at the same time every day, then do it. If connecting with nature feeds your spirit, that's fine.

We're all spiritual beings and when things go wrong we need somewhere to turn. For me, that means talking to God or the Divine Spirit, but I don't

say that's the only way. You may find peace by walking on the beach or gardening, by just being outside. I love being close to the sea. I can watch it for hours and it always makes me feel good inside and optimistic about life. Sometimes it's nice to go and sit in a church, just be there when no one else is around and have a quiet moment, to think and reflect.

When we don't have that in our lives, we start to feel like we're adrift and at times when we're stressed and under pressure, and there's too much going on, we can start to panic. Connecting with that anchor, touching base with the spirit, helps to stop the panic from taking hold.

Talk to God or whoever you pray to. Prayers don't need to be complicated or formal. They're about having a one-to-one conversation, seeking help and guidance, placing your trust in something else.

If you don't know how to begin, try something simple and direct like, 'You know what, I don't even know if you're there but I need you right now, so can you please just show me where I need to go?' That's all it takes.

Maybe you don't even want to pray. Just take the time out anyway, sit in silence, let your thoughts drift in and out, and ask the universe to tell you what you need to know. Trust me, you'll start getting answers.

Write things down – how you feel about your life, what you want to happen, the dreams you have. Putting pen to paper is such a powerful means of triggering change in your life. As soon as you express yourself in that way, you start to set things in motion. I do it all the time, make lists of the things I want to do and, as far as I'm concerned, the minute I write something down, I'm already saying it's going to happen. That's how much faith you have to have. Just try it.

Keep that piece of paper safe and when you feel you're losing your way take it out and remind yourself of your purpose and where you're going. Writing stuff down is a way of training yourself to have faith. When you have your list and you're ticking your goals off as you achieve them, you start to realise you were right to believe in the first place. You start to believe you're worthy of having good things happen in your life.

I really believe we are the creators of our own destiny, that we have the power to bring about change by our thoughts and actions, by having faith in ourselves and the universe. Whatever it is you want from life, a spiritual connection is going to help you get it because when your spirit is strong it gives you the determination and self-belief to carry on, no matter how bad things might look.

It's Not Looking Good

When I'm really going through hell I pray even more. I write down all the things I'm worried about and the way I'm feeling and I try to be an observer looking in on my own life. Writing about how I feel helps me offload some of the pressure and makes me feel less helpless and alone. I think for a lot of us the biggest fear is that we're on our own.

I might talk to my mum and my sister about why they think things are going wrong, try to get a bit of clarity, because when it's my own stuff I'm sometimes a bit blinkered, too close to get a clear view of what's really happening. I know my mum and my sister will be honest, tell me when I'm right or when I'm wrong, and that's exactly what I need.

Then I'll talk to God and ask for help. I'll just say, 'I'm not feeling good right now, I'm really hurting, and I don't understand why I'm not getting rid of these feelings. I know You're not going to give me anything I can't handle but I need You to help me through this one.'

Sometimes I get a voice that tells me to read something. The other day I picked up the Bible and the scripture I turned to was about how God is with humble people, which struck a chord with me. A lot of people had been telling me I'd been stupid about the choices I'd made, that I'd been a doormat in a lot of situations. I'd had people around me boasting and puffing their chests up and telling me how great they were, doing hurtful stuff. That scripture was about humility, not messing up, trying to be a good person, coming good in the end, and that's how I try to live my life.

I'm actually quite naive, quite green about people. If someone is smiling in my face and at the same time trying to deceive me, I probably won't see it because I'm not looking for it. They'll probably see that as me being a doormat, but that's okay because all those boastful people who were giving me a hard time have ended up with egg on their faces. That's always what happens; in the end they're the ones who will hang themselves.

I pray and I know I'm not alone, that nothing is all that bad after all.

No shrink can make me feel like that. I've tried and it doesn't work for me. I don't mean shrinks are a bad thing or that they're not right for other people, just that something intellectually led isn't going to give me the feeling of inner peace I get from prayer. I'm open to the idea of counselling, but it must have a spiritual basis.

I just find that when I'm unhappy, having a hard time of life, the quiet time I spend talking to God helps me make sense of things and gives me a feeling of being supported. I see the proof of God in my life in terms of what I'm led to do, not in any psychic sense, just a feeling inside that, regardless of what's going on and what's going wrong, something is looking after me. That's what having faith does.

Filling the Void

The panic and fear and helplessness that come when we're facing a crisis is just a form of energy swirling around inside, and it has to find an outlet. If it doesn't, we self-destruct. When there is no spirituality in our lives on any level, I believe there's a void and that we seek to fill it with destructive things.

I see my faith as a reserve that stops me from pressing the self-destruct button. It doesn't mean I won't ever go there, but I won't stay there because those things can't sustain me. I go out and have fun, have a few drinks, rave, and I go home and have my spiritual time.

I know a lot of drug addicts, tons of them, they go to work every day, some of them are on television, off their heads, and you don't even know it.

They have no spirituality and they're all filling the void with cocaine. That's what addiction is – a way of filling a void. If you have nothing to hold onto, no core, you try to escape into drugs, alcohol, sex, whatever happens to be your fix.

When people who have drug or alcohol problems go looking for help, the recovery is usually a 12-step programme that teaches spiritual principles. Those programmes can't work without a spiritual element and counsellors who work with addicts know that's an essential part of recovering from addiction. Put simply, surviving without spirituality can't be done.

So many times in my life I've had a sense of being take care of. In October, 1989, I was in San Francisco, driving through the city, over the Golden Gate Bridge, on my way to the airport, everything normal, people going home from work early because there was a big baseball game on that evening. The second our plane took off there was a massive earthquake and the city was absolutely devastated. More than 60 people died, thousands lost their homes, buildings and freeways collapsed. It was utter chaos. And I missed it by moments.

I wouldn't have coped with the situation with Andreas without God's help. I don't know how I was able to have the baby knowing he was cheating, living with someone else and their baby. I was broken, but I was also praying hard. Starting work on *What Not To Wear* three weeks after having Russia was the best thing I could have done, and I threw myself into it, heart and soul. I got that job when I was six months pregnant, when I wasn't even looking for it, and I believe it was God's way of putting something in place to help me cope when things crashed a few weeks later, just before Russia was born.

Whatever we choose to believe, one thing we can count on is that we definitely know what makes us feel good. I know when I'm doing the things that work for me because of the way I feel inside, and I know when I'm not because I feel completely lost. That's why I have faith.

What am I Doing with My Life?

The great thing about life is we can change it any time. We don't have to put up with anything we don't like. We don't have to stay with a guy who is making us miserable or do a job we don't like – it's up to us. It's our movie, remember, and we can re-write the script and change the action whenever we feel like it. The trouble is, a lot of people find the idea of change scary. Even when your life really isn't the way you want it to be, at least it's familiar. Change means stepping out of your comfort zone. It throws up uncertainties. It makes us feel unsure and insecure.

That's where faith comes in.

Maybe you haven't worked out your dream. Okay, what do you like doing? What are your hobbies, your interests, your passions? I was talking to someone recently who said they had no idea what they wanted to do with their life. When I did a bit of digging it turned out they were really into television. They loved their TV. I said, 'Okay, what is it you like so much about television? *EastEnders*? Right. So, do you want to be an actor? Do you want to be in TV production? How about working on the crew behind the scenes?' Suddenly, I could see something click. They'd never thought about it like that before but, yeah, actually, the idea grabbed them. You see what I'm saying? There's always something. It's just a case of finding it.

Trust in your judgement. Make the leap of faith. Ditching the dead-end job and doing the thing that makes you happy isn't easy. It takes courage, determination, and self-belief. You have to believe what your heart is telling you, even if everyone else is saying you're wrong. They don't think you can make a living out of photography? Fine. It's what *you* think that counts. Everyone thinks you're crazy to swap that nice regular salary for heaven knows what? That's okay, too. You're not trying to come up with a get-rich-quick scheme, you're just trying to fulfil your potential. You don't need to be obsessed with making money. You just need to be consistent with living your dream and the financial rewards will follow.

You have to *trust* in something bigger than yourself. You *know* the universe is going to take care of you, that you'll be provided for, come what may, and that's incredibly powerful. Whatever happens, there's a safety net in place. That's why faith is so massive.

Having a spiritual connection removes the element of doubt. It gives you the courage you need to take the plunge. It makes you realise that anything is possible. It also means that when the money does start to come in, you'll be in a position to appreciate it and enjoy the freedom it brings.

Fear should never hold you back. You're always going to feel it and the way to deal with it is not to let it debilitate you. Every time I go on stage I have a panic attack. Fear gets hold of me. I can feel it in my neck. I know that in the three minutes before I go on I'm going to feel terrible. I get so frightened. I worry the voice won't be there. I worry I'm not going to be good. I want to go out there and touch the people who've come to see me, but I'm afraid I'm going to let them down. It's the most horrible feeling and there's nothing I can do about it. Every single time I go out to sing that's what I go through. All I can do is hang on in there and pray to God that when I hit the stage, I'll be fine.

I could let it take me over, stop me from going on stage, but I don't. I just sit in the pain, get out there anyway, and *trust* that everything's going to be fine. Usually, by the second line of the song, it is, and the crippling sense of panic that was so real a few seconds earlier has completely gone.

I don't think fear and self-doubt ever go away. You can have the greatest gift, be outstanding at what you do, and still the fear is there. I've been listening to the Hawkins family since I was seven years old and what they do with gospel music just blows me away. Walter Hawkins is one of my great idols. His voice really affects me. The man is a legend, an absolute genius. He's been singing and performing all his life, so he knows he can do it but, like the rest of us, he has those moments of self-doubt. I saw him on TV not so long ago talking about his solo album and he admitted that putting himself out there, without the rest of the family around him, was making him nervous. Everyone feels fear but, in the end, you can't let it stop you.

When you're in a bad place, you believe that's all there is. You end up thinking you're stuck, that you have no real control, that there's only one way out. So, you get the woman who thinks the only answer is to find the rich guy, or the kid who thinks the only way he's going to make it is by selling drugs, or his mate who thinks the only way he's going to get respect is with a gun in his hand, or the girl who thinks the only way she'll feel better about herself is to bully the friend who's prettier than her.

There's always another way. There's always a choice. Unhappiness is an option. You can change it just like that when you start to fulfil your potential.

What Are You Waiting For?

Life really starts to take off when you play to your strengths, work out what it is you're really good at, and go for it. There's no point in working in a bank or on a supermarket checkout if what you're really good at is pottery. When I started out as a singer, I was doing backing vocals. I wasn't a solo artist, I didn't have a record deal, but I knew that's what I wanted. That was my passion. That was my dream. It never occurred to me not to go for it and I got there. I got a deal, everything took off – then I lost it. I got another deal, got busy again – then I lost it all. In between I had to get by as best I could and it was hard going, but I knew in my heart I was doing what was right for me.

I have no doubt in my mind that when you trust in the universe it provides for you in all kinds of unexpected ways. You're going to have your share of ups and downs, but once everything slots into place it's like winning the lottery. You hit the jackpot. Suddenly, you're in control of your own destiny. You have creative freedom, financial freedom. You're not waiting for someone else to give you the life you want. You already have it on your own terms. All of that starts with a dream.

I never put a time limit on anything I want to achieve. I think everything has its season. We have to learn to be patient. Every dream we have represents a seed. You have to take that seed and plant it, nurture it, wait for it to grow. It's going to take time.

You can't expect to see a harvest overnight so while you're waiting, you keep working on yourself, eating good food, keeping your body active, feeding your mind with positive thoughts, taking time out to pray and meditate.

Don't get mad when you feel like nothing is happening or other people are getting there ahead of you. It just means it's not your time – *yet*. There's a season for preparing, making plans, writing them down, working out where you want to go with your life. When you're in that lean patch and things are tough and nothing's really coming through, don't let it frustrate you or throw you off course. You just have to keep planting those seeds and reviewing your goals, because every time you do it's an act of faith. You're basically saying, I have faith – I believe I can do this.

> I never put a time limit on anything I want to achieve

Your season comes when the seeds you planted start to sprout. Usually, the most amazing things come along after the hardest times, so hold on in the storm and trust that when it finally passes you'll have your time in the sun.

Perfect Timing

Success doesn't always come just when you want it. After my *Black Angel* album in 1999 I thought I was finished, that I'd never sing again. Music was such a huge part of me, my first love, but it felt like it was over, gone for good.

What happened after that album, losing my deal, the record not being promoted, killed my spirit a bit. Singing has always made me feel like I'm on a different dimension. I've always looked on it as something amazing and powerful, a gift from God, and I felt I'd come to the end of the road.

It was so hard, but eventually I thought, 'God doesn't want me to sing right now,' and I had to let it go.

Then, early in 2007, I was approached to do a regular spot at Ronnie Scott's in London, and I jumped at it. On the first night I was absolutely terrified. It was something like four years since I'd done a concert. I was working with a band I didn't know and who didn't know each other, we hadn't rehearsed together – and I wasn't sure I could remember the words of the songs. I was so scared. The minute the music hit, though, it all came back and it was wicked, a really good night, very spiritual – and the song that really messed up the place was *Amazing Grace*.

The last time I sang at Ronnie Scott's had been 20 years earlier when I'd done a showcase for my first album, *So Good*. When someone in the audience shouted, 'Welcome back, Mica,' it felt like I'd come full circle.

It's great to be singing again, doing what I love, and I'm getting my confidence back. I think I'd forgotten I have a contribution to make to music and it's nice to have a reminder.

You'll sometimes find that when you're in a relationship one of you is getting all the breaks, all the good fortune, and the other one is struggling. It doesn't mean you're doing something wrong, it just means it's not your turn. Be patient. I went through that when I was with Andreas, banging my head against a brick wall, getting nowhere. I couldn't understand it. I was praying, planting the seeds, asking the universe to help me make my dreams come true, but nothing was coming through. People would say, 'What's going on – aren't you singing anymore?' I'd say, 'Yeah, I am, actually, you just don't see me.' I was going through a phase in my life where no one was interested and I couldn't get on television because it just wasn't my time. Then, suddenly, it all happened at once, *bam bam bam*. A TV series. A regular spot at Ronnie Scott's. A book. One after the other, just like that.

A Different Way of Being

Spirituality changes your outlook on life. You start to see yourself in a different light. You appreciate that what you do affects other people so you become more selfless, more compassionate, more aware. You're no longer going through life on auto-pilot, you're *conscious*.

Spirituality gives you a sense of being part of the universe, not just an insignificant dot on the landscape. You start to realise that your actions have consequences, that even the smallest things have an effect.

I think we're all connected, that whatever we do has repercussions. Once you start thinking like that you can't go round with a couldn't-care-less attitude, because you're aware of everything and everyone.

If I take a cab and give the driver a hard time, jump out, don't bother to thank him, slam the door and walk off without a word, how's that going to make him feel? How's he going to treat the next person that gets into the cab? If I'm patient, though, smile and say thank you, he's going to drive away feeling good. We all know how it feels when someone is nasty to us, how a few choice words can make us feel like crap, and how that can have a knock-on effect for the rest of our day.

The same goes for when something nice happens out of the blue – like a stranger paying you a compliment, being kind, giving up a seat on the bus, holding open a door. It can be something really small, but you're suddenly feeling good and someone else will benefit from your good experience.

Where I get my hair done there's a guy who makes the food and drinks. He does it really well and you can see he's taken the time to make the food look good on the plate. I talk to him, ask how he's doing, let him know I appreciate him, but what I've noticed is that most people don't even acknowledge him. They're on auto-pilot, so focused on what they're doing, so oblivious to what's going on around them, that they don't even see him.

The way I look at it, every time you give a little love and respect to another person – a smile, a few words of appreciation – you're blessing them with good vibes. And that means they'll do the same to the next person they meet, and it will all eventually come back to you.

Choices

No one makes the right choices all the time. We're only human and that means getting it wrong, messing up. We look back and think, 'Why in God's name did I do that? What was I thinking? How come I didn't see *that* one coming?' I definitely have days when I have a hard time coming to terms with some of the choices I've made. I think we all do.

The thing about life is it sets little traps. It's not plain sailing. There are always going to be hard times, times when it all goes wrong, and you don't feel optimistic anymore.

Having those moments, feeling down, is normal. I've been through that hundreds of times. It's nothing to be ashamed of. It's not a sign of being weak. When bad stuff happens, when you suffer disappointments and setbacks, of course you're going to feel bad.

I'm the eternal optimist. I always see the glass as half full. I know that, no matter how bad things are, they're going to get better in time. That's the way you have to look at life. Have your bad days – just don't collapse under the weight of them.

There are people who go through life thinking the odds are always stacked against them, that it doesn't matter what they do they're never going to be happy. They expect the worst. They tell themselves they'll never have any money, they'll always be in a dead-end job, they'll never meet the right guy… and on and on. And you know what? They're absolutely right. That's their movie. That's how they've set it up. It really doesn't pay to be pessimistic because the more you tell yourself that's how it is, the more that's how it's going to be. *What you think creates your reality.*

That's one of the biggest lessons we have to learn. If you want a happy, fulfilling life, it's up to you. We all have it in us to change our reality. When you start to embrace life and have an optimistic outlook it affects everything around you. All kinds of good things, opportunities you never dreamed of, start coming your way.

So, what do you do if you're one of life's pessimists? Simple – you change. You take the same approach that you would to anything.

You go home to yourself and do some work on your spiritual side.

Faith and spirituality aren't things we can ignore. They're part and parcel of making your life the way you want it to be.

We all know we have to look after our physical well-being. We know what happens if all we eat is junk food and never bother doing any exercise. The body gets overweight and unfit. We also know we can't starve the body because it needs good, healthy food to function well. We also have to feed the spirit.

Connecting with your spiritual side isn't an option as far as I'm concerned. It's something we all need to do. It's just an aspect of being in the best shape for life. Having faith, the act of taking time out each day to pray and focus, brings you closer to

> Having faith brings you closer to achieving your dreams

achieving your dreams. Time spent in your own company, thinking, meditating, writing down your goals, is a practical way of nourishing the spiritual element of yourself. You might not feel it right away but if you stick at it – just *trust* – you will notice the difference.

You'll start to feel that you have a place inside yourself to go when things are tough, that your spiritual connection is a comfort. When you're stressed and low and feeling helpless, those quiet moments can get you back on track. You'll start to get the answers to your questions, to work out where you've gone wrong in the past, and what you might do differently in the future.

Getting it Wrong

I'm the first to admit that my weakness has always been my relationships. I've never managed to get that bit of my life right, but that doesn't mean I never will. In fact, I feel more optimistic than ever about the future because I'm finally working out where I've gone wrong in the past.

I'm waking up to why I made the choices I did and I'm finding out all kinds of stuff about myself in the process.

I've started to see that I'm actually more emotionally dependent than I thought I was and how afraid I've been all my life of being abandoned – something I'd never picked up on before. It never helps to sit there and blame other people for what's gone wrong in your life. I think you have to get to the point where you just take responsibility. When something's not working for me, I want to know why. I have to go home, have that quiet time and connect with myself. I'm not looking for someone else to give me the answer. I know that until you take responsibility, you're just going to keep hitting the repeat button, doing the same stuff, until you get sick of it. Now, though, I've reached the point in my life where I'm ready to do something about it.

If I see the same guy coming along again – different look, same energy – I'm out of the door. I'm a sucker for a pretty face, always have been, but there's only so much good-looking you can take.

So now I'm looking for a different kind of guy, no-nonsense, real, and with a great spirit. I have no idea what he'll look like. It doesn't matter, though, because I've realised that you can be with a guy who's drop-dead gorgeous and a complete arsehole, and one day you look at him and you can't even see he's good-looking any more because his spirit is so ugly. Then there's the guy who's not good-looking at all, but is the nicest person, just a beautiful human being, and you fall in love with him. Every day that guy's going to look more handsome. That's the difference.

I'm on this learning curve right now and it's making me look at my own behaviour. Always going for the best-looking guy – what does that say about me? Surely, that's about *my* arrogance and *my* vanity?

I know I'm loud, love to party, have a good time – I've always been like that. Now, though, I'm starting to wonder how that looks. I'm taking a step back and thinking, what do *I* make of *me*? Am I a bit much at times? Am I too loud? Am I maybe a bit annoying? Okay, I don't mean to be, but is that how I'm coming across? Is that why I'm attracting showy guys all the time?

So, I'm working on that, going out and maybe not being the loud one.

What I went through with Andreas was excruciating, but I still thank him because, actually, I needed to work out what was going on in my life, question how I was doing things. It made me start looking at everything in my life and wonder, 'Am I in control, or am I letting other people do things for me?' I think it's very easy for us to throw things onto other people, especially the stuff we're not good at or don't like dealing with. I've always been terrible at the business side of things, no good at managing my money. I can see now how spoiled I was by the music industry, everyone running round doing everything for me. I just got used to it.

When I signed my deal with Island Records, I hadn't a clue about money. I just wanted to sing. It was the music that moved me, not the business side, so I just thought I'd leave all that to other people. It wasn't good, though, because I ceased to be in control and I carried on leaving that side of things to someone else for the next 20 years. At last I'm learning to be responsible and watch where the money goes, economise, budget, manage my finances, pay my bills myself, work on the business side of things – and it's good for me.

Wealth and Spirituality

I think some people are put off the idea of spirituality because they don't think it's compatible with wealth and material success. Actually, it is. All I say is if you want to really enjoy success and everything that goes with it, you have to be coming from a sound spiritual base. It's a mistake to think that money is a means to a great life. Get the great life first – then you can enjoy the money you make.

Your spiritual connection is going to give you an appreciation of wealth and help you build a solid financial foundation. I don't say you can't be successful without spirituality but, in my experience, it's a hollow kind of success.

Now, when I look back, I can see why things didn't feel right when I got my record deal and my career took off. I know why I had that sense of something missing, even though I was doing the thing I loved, singing and performing, having the success I'd dreamed of and living the most amazing life. The problem was, I had the wrong reasons for wanting it.

I'd been singing all my life and everyone told me I had a good voice, but things started to change the first time I got up and sang in front of a congregation at the New Testament Church of God in Brockley Rise, where my grandad was the minister.

I was about 13, we had people visiting that day, and my grandmother wanted to make a good impression so she told me to learn *God Will Open Doors*, a song by the American gospel group, the Hawkins family. I loved the Hawkins family's music and still do. So, that Sunday, I got up in front of everyone and sang and I'll never forget what happened. They all got to their feet and started clapping and just going mental. Then they asked me to do it again. I remember thinking, 'This time I'm really going to hold the notes long,' and the more I could see people being moved, the more I gave it. That's when I started to realise I had a gift, that there was something different about me, and that's when I started to become more confident.

The feeling of being able to touch people when I sang, that when I opened my mouth this sound came out, was such a great thing. For the first time in my life I felt special.

After that, my grandmother was amazing. She was like my agent, taking me to sing at all these different churches. We were getting invitations from all over the place. The Pentecostal Church is absolutely huge. When they have conventions they can fill a stadium the size of Wembley.

Whenever I sang it was like being taken over by another spirit, like something was coming through me from heaven knows where. I'd never had a tutor, never had vocal lessons, it was just there.

I've always felt humble about my voice because I didn't create it. The way I look at it, it's a gift from God and I'm so thankful to have it. I feel honoured that I can sing and that people like what I do.

There've been times when I've been sick with tonsillitis or laryngitis and my singing voice has still been there. One time I couldn't even speak and I had a big show to do in Holland. I went on stage, sang, came off, and *still* couldn't speak. I give thanks for it every day of my life.

Angry Young Woman

Once I'd been singing a couple of years, I started to rebel and get sick of the whole church scene. My hormones were raging, it was all going off, and I wanted to break out and leave church behind. I'd been doing it all my life and I'd just had enough. I was singing with a gospel group called the Spirit of Watts and I was starting to get more experimental with my music, doing gospel with a bit more funk in it, getting a bit more secular, but the others didn't like what I was doing.

I got angry, thinking, 'You guys have got a cheek telling me what to do – you're not perfect.' There was a lot of jealousy and bitchiness going on, people giving me a hard time for being good at singing, and I started kicking against it. It felt hypocritical and I wanted out.

I was so angry. Even though my grandparents had done a great job of raising me and my sisters, I was angry with my parents for not being around when I'd wanted them. I had all kinds of problems going on in my head. Because I was the youngest daughter I had a complex about that, thinking my older sisters were more important. I'd just never felt good enough, never felt like I was special.

I was angry with the church, angry with my family, and I wanted to prove I could make it and be this big success. I was on a mission thinking, 'I'll show you.' I wanted to say to everyone, all the people I thought had overlooked me or messed me around, all the friends who'd said I'd never make it – 'You see, I really *am* something.'

That was the driving force behind what I was doing and it was all wrong. My fuel was revenge, and it's the wrong energy, the wrong spirit if you want to enjoy your success when it comes. If revenge is driving you, you've pretty much had it. There was something else in my way, too, not that I knew it. I'd always had a strong spiritual connection through the church, but I decided I didn't need it anymore. I was wrong about that.

I was so angry with the church I got God confused with religion and turned my back on both, so, just as everything was taking off for me, I was in a bad place spiritually. I didn't think there was a place for spirituality in my life. I didn't think I needed it, but I've since worked out that, when it's missing, material success feels very hollow and meaningless.

I was counting on success to make me happy and I couldn't understand why it didn't. I was disappointed and frustrated. In my mind, I'd equated fame and fortune with feeling like a million dollars, thought it would make all the feelings of rejection go away, but if anything I felt worse. I had it all, but I felt like I didn't really have anything.

I really believe we all have to go after our dreams, but we have to follow them for the *right reasons*. I'm not saying you won't be successful if your motives are wrong, but I do know from experience there'll be a great, gaping void in your life.

It's Only Money

I don't see anything wrong in wanting to make money and have the material trappings of wealth – the nice house, the car, whatever you've set your mind on. What does bother me is being obsessed with wealth, when all that matters is materialism.

I think what's going on today is we respect *things* not people. When I was growing up we'd be impressed if someone was a doctor or a lawyer, but now we're impressed if someone drives a Ferrari. So, they drive a flash car, but what do they *do*?

I see so many wealthy people who seem to have it all, but they're absolutely miserable. It's just stuff. They have money, all the expensive toys they want, but nothing besides. No spirituality. Basically, we don't need lots of stuff to be happy. Mostly, having cars, boats, property, whatever it happens to be, is about letting other people know you have money. It's all, 'Look at me.'

It's best to travel light, have what you need and not be excessive. That way you can focus on the things that matter – doing great stuff, being fulfilled, having meaningful relationships – rather than worrying about possessions. Don't let money be the focus.

Years ago I met Peter Gabriel when I was recording at his studio on his estate near Bath, and I just thought he was amazing, one of those people you meet and straight away you can feel their presence. He blew me away. I looked at his life and he seemed to have got it just about right. He'd had all the fame and fortune you could imagine, sold millions of albums with Genesis, and it hadn't spoiled him or taken over his life.

He was still a nice guy, a normal person, enjoying what he'd earned without being a slave to it.

There's this whole thing going on now with everyone wanting to be famous and be all over the papers every day, but why would you? You have no life, you become obsessed with vanity and being seen, and then you get greedy because it's not enough. You don't just want to be in every magazine, you also want to be on TV, seen, recognised, photographed, talked about, and in the end that's all you care about.

There's no room for spiritual connection with all that going on, none.

I find it appalling that people who could be out there making a real difference actually choose to spend their time drinking champagne at £500 a bottle, getting wasted on drugs, and doing nothing more taxing than designer shopping. What is the point?

I remember when it all took off for me and the money started rolling in, I'd go shopping and buy a skirt that cost a grand. A thousand pounds on a single piece of clothing. I was 18 years old, had a massive advance from the record company, the music industry was awash with money in those days, and I got completely carried away with it.

When Monet was a baby I'd buy her clothes from this little French shop in Knightsbridge, pay £50 for a tiny little cardigan she'd grow out of in no time. I thought stuff like that was important. Now I look back and think it was complete madness. What a bloody idiot. You get a bit older, a bit wiser, and you start to work out what's really important. I couldn't spend that kind of money now and not feel guilty about it. I have different priorities.

I think people confuse wealth with happiness all the time. When you're struggling to make ends meet, living in a run-down place, yeah, of course money seems like the way out. And if you've got the cash you can change your life. Hit the jackpot, win the lottery, and you can have the mansion, the Ferrari, the celebrity lifestyle. But money doesn't give you the important stuff, the inner peace, the contentment, the sense of fulfilment. You have to get your relationship with yourself right first.

The more materialistic society gets, the more we need to get back to traditional values. People think that because we're in a technologically advanced age we no longer need old-fashioned values, but those values are what make us human. Remove them and we're screwed. What's happening is that the notion of moral fibre, right and wrong, selflessness, having a purpose – all that is seen as outdated.

When you've got the balance right, you don't just have the wealth, you also have contentment. You feel good. You don't need more than one car. You don't need a surgeon to make you feel good. You don't even notice that maybe your nose isn't perfect because that's not what's important. It's not what you're focusing on.

Contribution

I think we're all here to make a contribution to the planet in different ways and every single one of us can do something positive. Contribution is a personal thing. There are no hard and fast rules. Maybe you're not sure what you're meant to be doing. Maybe you don't think you're doing enough. Maybe you don't think you're doing anything and you're not sure where to start.

I actually believe that contribution starts with taking care of yourself and getting your own life in shape, before you start doing stuff for other people.

The more work you do on your spirituality, the clearer an idea you get of what else you're meant to be doing in terms of your contribution to your environment and the people around you.

When you're coming from a good place, your heart is compassionate and your spirit is clean, you're constantly contributing good things. You don't even have to think about it. You just have a great positive energy that people pick up on and that in itself makes a difference. We all know how it feels to be around people who are full of life and optimism and enthusiasm. They make us feel good. They raise the spirits of everyone they meet.

I'm a great believer in enthusiasm. It's infectious, it catches on. I have a real love of people and I love life. That's just how I am. I'm not faking it. When I go out I am the life and soul because I want everyone to have a great time. I want people to feel good around me.

I've always been the way I am today – passionate, outspoken, spirited – and it hasn't always served me well. When I signed to Island Records 20 years ago, I faced the executives in the boardroom and sounded off about making a record that would stand the test of time. I was full of it, a skinny kid, just starting out, telling the guys in suits what I was going to do. I had this, 'I know who I am and I know what I want,' attitude. The truth was I was really scared, but I cared so much. I wanted to do great things, not be mediocre, and a lot of people took it the wrong way. They didn't think I was passionate about my music; they just thought I was arrogant and difficult.

I remember doing a radio interview in the States and Robert Palmer heard it. I'd never met the guy, but he took offence at something I said and complained to Chris Blackwell, who ran Island. I got an absolute roasting and I can't even remember what it was about, but I was always getting told off, usually because people kept trying to label me the next Whitney Houston and I wouldn't go along with it. No disrespect to Whitney – she was the Queen – but I could only be *me*.

The thing is people aren't always going to 'get' you, but you can only be true to yourself. You can only do the thing you think is right. Even when I was a kid I was always questioning stuff, always had an answer. In Jamaica they call it *face-tee*, which means being cheeky, having a lot of front, and I do, I know, but that's just me. I'm exactly the same now as I was when the record company was telling me off for having too much to say – only now people like it. What was once perceived as arrogance has become strength of character. I wanted to go all the way with my music, use my voice to really connect with people, and that's how I am with everything I do. I follow my heart. I'm like that with my relationships, my friendships, my parenting. I'm deep, I go all the way. For me it's all or nothing, no grey areas.

I think being conscious, having a deep spiritual connection, leads you to become more in tune with the universe. You start to develop a bit of a sixth sense. Something 'tells' you to pick up the phone and call someone you haven't spoken to for ages and you find they really needed to hear from you. You take a different route to work and bump into someone you haven't seen in a while who's going through something major in their life and really needs someone to talk to.

You just keep finding yourself in the right place at the right time. I don't think that's coincidence. I think that's what happens when your life is working smoothly, when you become more understanding, more receptive – more *aware*. That's how it works.

That's how you start making the contribution you're meant to. When I was younger my contribution was more about touching people with my music. Now I think that's just a part of it. I'm on a mission now to encourage women to be strong, to believe in their uniqueness and their beauty, to realise they have a purpose, that they have the power to change their life – and to go for it.

That's what I think I'm meant to be doing with my life. I'm not saying it's easy and claiming I get it right all the time. I struggle with my shit every day, but I do know from experience what works for me, what helps me get through the painful stuff, what keeps me on the right track. And I know I wouldn't be where I am without having faith and spirituality.

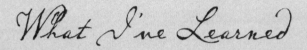

What I've Learned

- My faith has given me optimism through the sad times
- Showing kindness and appreciation of others will reap rewards
- Set aside time to think, pray, meditate – it keeps you grounded
- We all have it in us to change our reality

Life & Death

My brother Jason was shot dead six years ago.

A guy had been hassling his girlfriend, thrown a bottle at her, and Jason went to his house to speak to him. He was shot three times and died on the pavement. He was 21 years old.

It was Valentine's Day, 2001, and I was just about to take my daughter, Monet, and my niece, Cherice, for lunch when I got a call from my sister, Paula. When she told me Jason was dead it didn't sink in. I said, 'What do you mean? He's *hurt* himself?'

'No,' she said, 'he's dead.'

When someone you love suddenly dies it's always a shock, but when their life is snuffed out with such violence it's the most horrible thing. Jason was so young, such a beautiful guy, going about his life in a quiet way, working as a postman, bringing up two beautiful children. Then, one day, no warning, he's dead.

The guy who shot my brother had no respect for life. He was prepared to kill just like that. He left Jason's children without a father and our family broken, just torn in pieces. And why? Because he'd tried to make a move on my brother's girlfriend and she'd turned him down. All Jason wanted to do was put a stop to it, but he came up against someone who didn't think twice about pulling the trigger.

It was a terrible, traumatic time for all of us. When someone dies in that way it completely obliterates the family. No one knows who to blame, who to talk to, what to say, how something so senseless can happen in a street in south London in broad daylight. It's total madness.

I could see everyone around me falling apart, especially my mother, and I was afraid Jason's murder would kill her, too. She wanted to die, to be with him – no ifs or buts or maybes – that's how she felt. We practically had to drag her away from the cemetery.

I don't think people understand what it means to lose someone you love in such shocking circumstances. They don't see the damage it does, what happens to the people left behind. It's all over and done with too quickly: guy shoots, boy dies, mother on telly crying, bit of a march, end of story. The media moves on while the family tries to pick up the pieces.

What's Going On?

When Jason died I was so caught up with trying to keep the rest of the family going I don't think I actually grieved properly, until much later. I saw myself as the one who had to push everyone else, make them feel things could get better. It's what I always do and, in the past, when I've crashed, they've done the same for me. My mother was in a really bad way, just falling down, and I couldn't let myself fall with her. I was just thinking I had to get her out of there. She was going to the cemetery all the time, just about living there, and it was dangerous, so I had to pull her back.

Our family was ripped to shreds, totally annihilated, and I didn't want other families going through the same thing, so I went on the warpath.

Jason's death opened my eyes to what was going on in the black community. The day he was shot two other guys were also killed. It was happening all the time but no one was paying any attention. Nobody cared. I had no idea how much violence and murder was happening because I was living the good life. Being a pop star had taken me out of that world, away from neighbourhoods like Croydon and Brixton where people were being shot and stabbed.

I'd moved to a nice part of town, spent my time flying all over the world, making my music, operating in a different sphere. I just didn't know what was going on in the world I'd left behind, but once I found out I felt I had a responsibility to make other people aware, too.

I didn't actually want to speak out on gun crime. I wasn't comfortable with the idea of being some kind of spokesperson. It actually frightened the life out of me. I just thought it was too much to take on and I was afraid of getting it wrong. I thought – 'I don't go on television and speak my views. I'm a singer, not a politician.' I was scared it would get me into trouble.

I'm honest, painfully so, known for putting both feet in my mouth, and the thought of saying the wrong thing, hurting people – especially the ones who'd already lost someone – made me want to run the other way. I just thought there was no way I could do it. I didn't feel I was up to it. I was a bit intimidated.

Politicians practise for years. Their vocabulary alone is amazing, and the way they answer questions is so structured, so tailored. I thought, 'Me – tailored? The only thing tailored about me will be my suit.' There's no way I could ever tailor my thoughts or my answers, have someone ask me a question and think, 'I'll avoid giving them a straight answer by going somewhere else with this.'

But a lot of people wanted me to speak out and I could feel it. My mum wanted me to be vocal because she needed people to see that her son's life was worth something, and she was absolutely right about that. I had other mothers who had lost their sons saying, 'You've got to be the one to do this.' And all the time the media was clamouring for something.

I spoke to my sister Paula about it. 'It's too much, P, I've got this overwhelming fear. This is massive, man, I can't do it. It's too powerful.'

She gave me this look she has and said, 'Listen, Michelle, God has given you this opportunity to make a difference – you *must* do it.'

She was right, but I was so scared and emotionally raw. Jason had just died and I was thrust into the media spotlight overnight. Somehow I held myself together, although I've no idea how. I just had to. Throw me in at the deep end and I'll always swim.

I was used to press and television, but not like this. Suddenly I was on *Newsnight*, Sky, the *Six O'Clock News*, and the story just ran and ran. I spoke on the radio, gave newspaper interviews, did every damn thing I could. And I said what I felt, didn't try to dress it up. Then I got involved with Trident, the Metropolitan Police campaign to tackle gun crime in the black community.

That was how I coped with Jason's death – by trying to do something. Even when things are about as bad as they can be that's how I have to be. It's the only way I know.

Make a Difference

I always deal with my pain by trying to make a difference, doing something to try and stop other people suffering in the same way. My whole focus was about shielding other families from the pain we were going through.

I wanted to know what was going wrong, why these young black boys were killing each other, and I wanted to do something about it. It's the only way to deal with such a massive loss. Do what you can to help someone else and that way you stop internalising your feelings and letting the same negative stuff get hold of you until it sends you off your bloody head.

What I saw going on in the black community six years ago made me think that if no one talked to these boys the violence was going to become an epidemic. It's like society is willing to let black girls in but not black boys, so they end up feeling ostracised, thinking no one really cares, that people are sneering at them because they're black.

The media portrays them as thugs and thieves and hoodies. They're out in the cold with no sense of pride, no self-worth. I don't think it's the fault of the kids that they're a mess. The family unit is in bits, there's no home life, no feeling of safety and security. People have forgotten how to parent their children.

In early 2007 there was a spate of shootings in south London. In the space of two weeks, three young black boys were shot and killed. The third one to die, 15-year-old Billy Cox, was shot in his bedroom on Valentine's Day – the sixth anniversary of my brother, Jason's, death. Six years on and it's still happening, families going through what we went through, young lives snatched away.

And I'm working with Trident again, still hoping to make a difference. Someone asked me recently if making it illegal for 16-year-olds to carry guns would make a difference and I said no. It's like putting a Band Aid on a broken leg. What difference is that going to make? We've got to go back to the home because it's broken. We've got to teach parents how to parent. Children are joining gangs because they have no family structure.

Sometimes it's like the parents don't even know their kids – there's a real stranger vibe going on. So the kids make the gang their family unit and gun culture makes them feel they're somebody in a society that has made them feel rejected.

I want these young boys to feel a sense of pride, to believe they can be giants, and it has to start in the home with good, conscious parenting. Parents need to be taught how to create a safe home for their children, how to be good role models, how to stop their kids looking for a sense of belonging on the streets.

Survival of the Fittest

If I looked at my kids and felt I was losing them, I'd fight for them, and that's what we all have to do. Life is about fighting for the things you believe in, and to survive you have to be fighting fit.

Parents can't relax and wait for someone else to be the role model. Why should a footballer be your child's role model? It has to be *you*. And I think when you're working on yourself, becoming more conscious, trying to be a good person, operating on a spiritual level as well as a material one, you're setting the best example you can for your kids. They're going to be the benefactors because they'll copy you and that way they'll become great human beings.

I'm comfortable now about being an ambassador for Trident and speaking about gun crime and what's going on in our communities. I'm not perfect in any way and I don't think I know it all, but I'm not so afraid of messing up and saying the wrong thing anymore. I just think, 'Guess what, you're going to screw up sometimes because you're only human.'

I make many mistakes, but I don't think people mind when they know that you're honest and straight and your intentions are honourable. All I'm trying to do is find practical solutions and I don't think it matters that I'm not a politician. In fact, I think sometimes conventional leaders don't have a real feeling for what people need. You see it all the time on television debates where the politicians are facing an audience and have not the slightest feeling for what that audience really wants.

Life is about fighting for the things you believe in

One of the things about singing is that you pick up on the mood of your audience right away. You can tell when people are hostile and you know how to break that and reach them through the music. I think we're in an age where people are looking for different kinds of leadership, not just the intellectual kind with no spiritual context, but something deeper that's more in tune with their feelings.

We're going to see different kinds of leaders coming through, getting more vocal, challenging the accepted way of doing things, and they won't be the types that went to Harvard or Oxford or Cambridge. It won't be academic qualifications that matter in the future, it'll be emotional intelligence.

The Ultimate Wake-Up Call

Death is the big one. When someone you love dies you can either die with them or decide to really live and do something with your life. It's the ultimate wake-up call. That's how it's always been for me. It's like life getting hold of you and going, *come on.*

Jason's death was a huge turning point in my life. My conversations with God at that time were really intense. What I got spiritually from that whole episode was the feeling I had to get on top of things, do more with my life. The pain of losing my brother gave me a real sense of urgency about life and made me feel I had to do more than just mourn his death.

Death shakes me up, makes me realise nothing is to be taken for granted, that life can all be over in a second and, suddenly, all those great things you were going to do didn't happen. I cry and I grieve for the person I've lost, but at the same time I know I can't go with them, and that I have to get my act together, get out there, and get on with it. My God, death is a big one, but you can't let it debilitate you. You can't let it kill you.

Life is about surviving, so you have to find a way to feel sad and say goodbye, to feel the pain of missing the person you've lost, and move on. The way I feel about death is down to how I was brought up. I was taught to value people while they're here, make the most of them, and I really believe in that. My grandparents always used to say, 'Give people their flowers before they die,' and that's what I try to do.

When that's how you live, it eases the pain of losing someone you love.

If you fall out, and someone dies before you've had chance to make it up, it's much harder. I've met people who feel eternal guilt for not putting things right when they had the chance, and it becomes something that eats away at them forever.

I think it all comes back to being a conscious human being, treating people the way you want to be treated, always being as good as you can be.

I don't want to lose someone and think the last time I was with them I was a total bitch, that I made them feel like shit. I want to make people feel good, to leave a good taste, because that's how *I* want to feel. When you're conscious of other people's feelings, you're less likely to create situations where there's bad stuff left hanging in the air. It's just not worth it.

When you hold onto grievances, it's always harder to grieve. The way I see it, if you fall out with someone you love, you have to mend it – for their sake and yours. Just deal with it, sort things out, because they might not be here tomorrow. That way, you live a life that's guilt-free, that means you can come to terms with death, grieve and have good memories, not feel angry and cheated, wishing you'd done things differently forever.

That's Not All There is

I don't see death as final. I've never had that view. I've always felt it's transitory, about going to another level, another aspect of existence – something we're all going to do. I don't believe that when you die it's all over: The End. That's what my faith has taught me and, when you see it that way and take the finality out of death, it no longer stings you so badly.

I see the universe as something that changes and evolves, where everything has its lifespan, where we all have our time and then move on to the next phase. However painful it is to lose someone, I believe that's how long they were supposed to be here. I think there's an order to what happens in life, that there's a reason for what we go through, the good things and the bad.

When my cousin died, I was just 17, making my first album. He was my best friend, the guy I hung out with, a total nutter who made me laugh so much, and then one day he wasn't there. He was never going to be there again. I was so devastated I wanted to go with him, jump in the grave, but I knew inside that's not what he would have wanted. He'd have said go out and kick arse with my music – and that's what I did. His death sent me into overdrive, made me even more focused, made me realise whatever time we have is precious. That was what losing my cousin taught me and I've been like that ever since.

Anyone who's had a near-death experience has that same sense of wanting to make every moment count. They've got a second chance and they're on a mission. I think we need to cultivate that same sense of urgency so that we get the most from life. A lot of people are too relaxed, especially the new generation of kids, just waiting for things to be handed to them on a plate. We shouldn't need a near-death experience to appreciate what we have; we should already have that enthusiasm for life, that sense of 'I've got to get on with things because I don't know how long I'm going to be here.'

I see death as something to spur me on, not break me, and feeling like that helps. It eases some of the pain.

There's not a day goes by I don't think about my brother, but time is a great healer. You never forget, but you do become better at dealing with the hurt. When Jason was shot it ripped the family to shreds and we've been through a tough few years but, gradually, there's been a coming together. Our relationships have changed. We know the value of each other. We take nothing for granted. We will never allow a fight to get out of hand. When something goes wrong, we fix it. Things are really good between us now – and that has something to do with Jason not being here anymore.

I think we all need to get more comfortable with the way we deal with death and working on your self-awareness gives you a different, less fearful perspective. I've done a lot of research, read accounts of near-death experiences, and it's incredibly reassuring. It's the not knowing, the uncertainty of what happens next, that freaks a lot of people out. I actually don't feel like that. I don't think there's anything to be afraid of, but I've spoken to people who say, 'I hate God for taking that person from me. I'll never get over it.' They really believe that's it, you die, kaput, there's nothing more. I'd say just listen to what the near-death experience people have to say and you'll never be the same. It's like a smoker going onto a ward where people are dying from cancer and emphysema. You get the message, and the more work you do the less fear you have.

I don't know why Jason's life was taken or why there's so much evil in the world, but I can say one thing; I was never the same again. His death gave me a push, told me I had to do things differently, that I couldn't go back to what I was. It made me want to live life to the full. Sometimes that's a bit scary, but there's something to be said for taking on the things that scare you, for living life by the seat of your pants – because that's when you do your best work.

What I've Learned

- You should be the role model for your children
- Take on things that scare you – that's when you do your best work
- 'Give people their flowers before they die'

Now What?

When I was a teenager, I thought I knew it all.

I had an answer for everything. I don't feel like that anymore. The older I get, the more I realise I have so much to learn. I have a huge thirst for knowledge, a need to find things out, to soak up information. I'm always looking for answers, constantly reading, delving into stuff that fascinates me, always questioning, researching, wanting to know more.

The older I get, the more aware I am of how little time we have on earth and that makes me think, 'Come on, man, you have to get busy.'

I'm on a journey, searching for answers every day of my life, but I feel I'm finally in a place where I'm happy and more contented than I've ever been. I know who I am, what I'm about – and I'm comfortable with it. I'm not scared of being on my own anymore. I'm not afraid of not being liked. I'm confident, *really* confident, whereas before I was just acting it. There have been countless times in the past when I've said I love who I am because it sounded good, but I haven't meant it. I don't really know why it's so hard for us to love ourselves, but appreciating who we are is something most of us struggle with every day of our lives.

Now, I can see real changes in myself, both outside and in, and I know it's because of the work I do every day to keep my mind, body and spirit fit and healthy. I still feel I have such a long way to go, that life is a work in progress, and you don't ever hang up your hat. There's always more to be done to be a good girlfriend, a good wife, a good parent, a good sister, a good friend. There's no room for arrogance. The minute anyone thinks they know everything, they're already finished.

I'm not saying my way is the only way, or the best way, but I know from experience that it works.

- When you make a conscious effort to take care of yourself, work on your awareness, have a spiritual connection, and do your best to fulfil your potential, your life definitely changes for the better.
- Once you start doing the work you have a different view of yourself and the world. You become more at ease, more balanced, more in tune with other people.
- The more conscious you become, the more you find out about the real you. It's like peeling the layers off an onion until the whole thing is revealed.

That's how I feel, that one after another the layers come off and I'm getting to see what's really going on inside, what my strengths are, and my weaknesses.

I Think I Get it

When I was 17, launching a career in pop, I was choosing the boys to be in my videos, picking the best-looking ones – and that's what I've been doing ever since in my relationships. Always falling for the ones with the looks instead of the ones who've got it all going on inside, blind to the stuff I can't see.

Now I've realised it's time to get a grip and not be so into the look. I can't go out with someone anymore just because they look good. It's not enough. I want someone who's intellectual *and* spiritual, a man who's a seeker, who's constantly learning and evolving. My God, that would be the jackpot.

It's taken me a long time to like being on my own because I'm a real social animal. I come from a huge family. My mum had six children, my grandmother had eight, and we were all living in this big Victorian house together. You can imagine how funky that place was. So my whole life was full of action and when the time came for me to be on my own and find out who I really was it was hard.

Going home to myself and facing my loneliness was the best thing I ever did, though. We all have to do it. You get such a sense of peace. Now, I love having time to myself. I need it. I've just started learning to go away on my own, which is something I'd never have done in the past, but I absolutely love it.

I don't need to be out, around other people for the sake of it. I'm happy going home to Russia, sticking a bottle in her mouth, talking baby talk, giving her a big kiss and putting her to bed. I say my prayers, have a bath and I'm gone. I just want a guy to come along and be exactly the same, to have worked on his stuff the same way I have, and that's it, done. No drama, not anymore. That's who I am now and some people are going to find that very boring but that's okay. I think too often we worry about what other people think and the truth is, as long as you're living your life right, it doesn't matter. What's more important is that your immediate environment – your family and friends – is good. Is it productive? Does it serve you? Do you need to make changes to filter out the things that aren't working for you?

I'm not so affected by the opinions of others anymore – unless they're people I really care about. If Monet turns round and says, 'Mum, I really don't like that song,' that affects me. But if some guy in the press says he hates it, I just think, 'Oh well, I liked it – maybe he'll like the next one.' I think you can become a slave to what other people think. People are always going to have their opinions and that's fine. Just don't let them kill you. Keep other people's opinions in perspective. Focus on the people that really matter to you. Make sure you have positive people in your life, all working towards the same thing, characters who make you feel you can be anything you want to be.

And don't let anyone fool you –
- The hardest thing in life is not making money.
- The hardest thing in life is not becoming successful.
- The hardest thing in life is having good people around you.

It's taken me 20 years to find people who love me and are totally dedicated, whose interest isn't monetary. When it's just about the money, it doesn't feel good. I've had more managers than hot dinners – sacked them, reinstated them, sacked them – and now I manage myself. I have a PR guy and a lawyer and that's it.

You can tell when it's from the heart and someone is really into being with you, wants to work with you and be a partner in your dreams. That's how it has to be – working together for a shared goal. When that's how it really is you feel it. When it's only about money you feel that, too, and you have to get out. You can smell those people. The truth always smokes them out. What I notice is I start feeling uncomfortable around them and, as time goes by, either I pull away or they do.

The thing about being on this journey is that you lose people along the way. Once you decide you want to change your life and you're becoming the being you're destined to be – fearless, living from your passion, caring for other people, making time for you and for God – everything changes.

Some people want you to crash and it doesn't matter how kind or loving you are with them, the more success you have the less they're on your frequency. It's disappointing, but sometimes you just have to let it go and focus on what you're here to do.

Nelson Mandela said we shouldn't come down from the mountain to meet the people – we should make them come up to us. When you're on top of that mountain in utopia there are going to be people who'll want to drag you down to where they are, but you don't have to go. You just have to stay where you are, not worry about them, and they'll either come up to meet you or they'll fall away.

You'll get to see who's there for you and who isn't, though, that's definite. It's not about being arrogant or aloof, it's about following your heart, doing what's best for you.

Usually, we know what feels right, but we don't always trust our instincts. I'm getting better at doing that, although I still get it wrong – I meet people, get a bad feeling, talk myself into going along with them anyway, and, down the line, end up going – you idiot, you *knew*.

More and more, though, I can feel when someone's being genuine and when they're not. They might have all the right answers, but if something isn't right it shows and you end up thinking, 'You know what, just be real – or leave.'

We all spend too much time doing things because we think we should, not because we want to, because we feel under pressure to go with the herd. I simply don't do the things I don't want to anymore. I don't go to places I don't want to. Why would you? You're just going to end up stressed and unhappy, drinking too much because you're not having a good time. What's the point? You could have stayed in reading a good book or having some spiritual time, or you could have gone to the gym, had a sauna, been for a run, but instead you chose to go somewhere, knowing you didn't actually want to be there.

We do it all the time. 'Oh, so-and-so's having their barbecue, the one they have every year, and I really don't fancy it, but I have to go.'

'Why do you have to go?'

'Oh, well, if I don't everyone's going to be saying stuff and I'll feel bad.'

'Why will you feel bad?'

'Well, I don't want them saying stuff about me.'

And that's it? *That's* why you're going to make yourself be somewhere you hate, where you always have a crap time and wish you hadn't bothered.

It's just not justifiable, cow-towing to what other people want you to do. Learn to trust your feelings, live by your truth, do the things that make you feel good – and forget the rest. We're all too easily influenced and thrown off course by other people and that's why it pays to know why you're here. It pays to find out what your passion is and develop an unshakeable belief in who you are and your purpose in life. The worst thing you can say is, 'I don't know what I want to do.'

That says you haven't dealt with yourself, haven't checked out who you really are or where you're going. It's code for, 'I don't know who I am.'

There are opportunities out there for everyone, but not everyone is going to see them. It's a bit like having a garden with lots of treats hidden in it and all you see is withered trees. That doesn't mean the treats aren't there – it's just that you can't see them. We have to change our perception. It's like listening to Radio 1. Just because that's all you're hearing doesn't mean Radio 2 doesn't exist. There are too many people stuck on one radio station, thinking that's all there is, not knowing there are many more out there. *You* have to change *your* frequency if you want to tune in to all the great things the universe has to offer.

Meant to Be

I believe that everything I've gone through over the years has been preparation for whatever's coming next. The pain and the suffering, the headaches, the ups and downs, having too much, not having enough, bankruptcy, losing friends, bad relationships, hating myself, and all the other stuff – it's all made me the person I am now.

I always thought I was a singer, only a singer, and that was all I was meant to do. Now, though, I feel like I'm being prepared to do so many other things. I've written this book, presented TV and radio shows, and taken on things I've never done before. And it feels right, like this is how my life is meant to be. I feel we're in a time where we have to be honest about who we really are. When you're doing the work on yourself, coming from a conscious place, you start to see where you've come from, the setbacks you've had, the mistakes you've made. It makes you a more compassionate person, the kind of person who gives a shit about everybody else, and feels a duty to help other people and tries to make a difference.

That's what I'm supposed to do, I know it. That's my mission. I was sitting the other day thinking I've been so judgmental in the past and I sometimes still catch myself being like that. It's not good. We really have to watch ourselves because that's the ego, the most destructive thing, trying to get the upper hand.

I've been hurt, had some nasty things done to me, but I can't say I'm innocent, that there isn't someone somewhere who has been hurt by me in the past. With awareness, though, you try to prevent it from happening in the future. I just think that those who hurt people are hurt themselves, and that when you fix the hurt, whatever it is, you stop harming others.

I'm very conscious now of not wanting to hurt anybody. I'm at home with my feelings and I love people. I'm not a victim anymore, not loving because I'm expecting something back, not loving in the hope of changing people, just accepting them for what they are and loving them anyway. That's what love is meant to be – unconditional.

I love being around people who make me feel good and that's what I try to do. If I can make you feel great, bring something positive into your day, that's what I'm going to try to do. If that's your focus, doing something that brings joy to others, you'll always be happy.

I know what it means to feel appreciated, I'm super aware of that. Most people never get appreciation and the minute I sense that I try to do something about it. It's really important. Just engaging with somebody, giving them a bit of your time, a few kind words, can make a real difference. You might give that person renewed hope, make them feel life's worth living after all, stop them from going home and taking an overdose. Being aware, creating good vibes – always doing what you can to leave something positive behind – takes such a small effort. The worst thing we can do is leave a bitter taste in somebody's mouth.

I'm really sensitive, like a walking nerve, and I definitely feel it when people aren't nice. If you're not strong inside, the way a person treats you, how they speak to you, can debilitate you. It's like being fed poison, and when you take it and eat it, it seeps into every part of you and slowly kills you. Every time someone pushes that same button again it's another dose of poison straight into the vein.

A few years ago I was in my car and someone drove into the side of me. I ended up with whiplash in my neck and shoulder. What I couldn't

understand was that the pain kept coming back, that every time I was a bit run down, or around the time of the month, that pain was right there again. Then a physiotherapist told me that the body records events and damage in the same way as a camera, storing the image in the cells, and replaying it. Every detail stays in your personal archive forever and the body just keeps on regurgitating it. It's the same when people say something that's nasty and you take it in – 'I hate you. You make me sick. I can't stand you.'

All that stuff leaves a lasting imprint and the more you dwell on it, the more damage it's going to do. When you go on and on about your pain, bringing it up every chance you get, reminding yourself of how bad it made you feel, it's only yourself you're hurting. The person who gave you the poison isn't even thinking about you anymore. When something bad happens you know it, you know who hurt you, but you don't have to let it take over your every waking thought.

I think one of the reasons people hang onto pain is because they don't understand where it goes. They don't think it's important until it kicks them in the face. Every time you dwell on the thing that hurt you, you're taking another step along the road to depression.

That's how it begins. You become a victim. You feel hard done by. You start hating your life, feeling miserable and bitter. You don't go out and see friends, you sit at home drinking, smoking, watching TV, killing yourself slowly. That's why it doesn't pay to do it. The body is taking notes at a cellular level and that's why we have to be so careful and watch what we do to one another.

We have to train ourselves not to obsess about the stuff in the past that hurt us, not to dwell. I love the Jim Carrey movie, *Eternal Sunshine of the Spotless Mind*, and the idea of erasing bad memories. We have to train ourselves to do that, let go of the pain, and live each day like it's our first.

When Pain Makes You Sick

I believe that people get sick when the body is ill at ease, stressed out, bombarded with negativity. It's poison and it does serious damage. All disease, all sickness, is to do with the conscious state. How you feel dictates how your body functions. If you feel like shit and there's a cold going round, you can bet you'll get it and if you start taking it on, thinking it's not just a cold, that you've really got flu or maybe even pneumonia, you're just going to feel worse and worse.

When you're feeling good that same cold is going to be a sniffle that's gone in no time. It comes back to being a victim. When that's how you feel and you're dwelling on it and everyone around you is encouraging you to feel bad, it's like a cancer inside.

When I go to my grandmother and say, 'Oh he did me wrong,' she just looks and me and says, 'Ah, relax yourself, Michelle.' She's seen it all, been there, worn the T-shirt and she just knows it's all going to pass. That's the kind of wisdom you get from old people, but we don't have to wait to be 80 to see life the way they do. We can be like that now if we choose.

I think we have to live knowing that everything we do, everything we say, affects everybody else, that every thought, every action has a consequence. If we could *see* what our thoughts actually do – see just how powerful our thoughts are, and see the damage one negative remark can do – I think we'd all be a lot more careful.

When you're working on yourself the negative stuff ceases to be so important. It's there, but it's not going to destroy you. What happens is you still hear it when someone's nasty, you're still conscious of it, but it no longer has the power to drag you under. The work is so engrossing, so intense, that you stop obsessing about the other stuff.

There is so much negativity in this world that I have to have a faith-based system of living. There is simply no other way for me. I've tried to get by without a spiritual connection, but that feeling of fighting and being on your own is too tiring.

The Old Man in the Rocking Chair

I still have a voice in my head that nags me, tells me I'm rubbish, why do I bother... all that. My dad used to call it the old man in the rocking chair and I know it's always going to be around.

We all have that going on, self-doubt, lack of confidence, a fear that we're crap really. I hear the old man in the rocking chair most days – 'You're this, you're that, what are you doing with yourself?'

I used to have a real battle with it, have those times when I got so down, so blue and hurting, being a victim, but now I know how to deal with the voice. I know how to turn down the volume, not let it get to me.

We all get those dark days, but now when they come they're not so scary because I know I don't have to obsess about them, feel like I'm going into a deep valley and I'm never going to come out.

Setbacks, disappointments, crises – you didn't get the job, the guy you want doesn't want to be with you, someone you love dies – those things are all part of being human. Bad situations will always come along, but it's not what happens, it's *how you react*. The key is not to let events overwhelm you.

You're going to have doubtful times when you're in that valley, that pit of depression, feeling lost and low and like you're never going to feel good again, but it's just a phase. The bad times are there so that we know when things are good. How are you ever going to know the good stuff if you've nothing to compare it with? You have to go through it to know it.

It's **not what happens**, it's how **you react**

What we do is make the mistake of thinking the bad times are going to last forever. We get scared because we think that's all there is. We all do it. How many of us, though, when we're in a good, happy place in our lives believe *that's* how it's always going to be? When things are going well we're afraid it won't last, that something's bound to come along and burst the bubble. We know the good times don't last forever, that they come and go. It's the same with the bad times. They come and go, too.

The trick is to get into the habit of reminding ourselves that everything – good and bad – is temporary. So when you're in that valley, keep giving yourself that message. *It's temporary.* Write it down. Stick it on your desk, on the mirror in the bathroom, the bedside table, anywhere you're going to see it, and keep repeating it; *it's temporary.*

In time, the bad things don't even get to you in the way they once did because you see them for what they are – events that will pass.

It's Your Life

Every day we're learning how to manage our emotions and not to let them dominate. That doesn't mean getting rid of negative feelings – it means handling them in the right way. The only way to be in control and free is not to be ruled by your emotional state and it's a balancing act – a question of finding the means to control your emotions without being a cold person. If you can control your emotional state, you'll be controlled in the way you treat yourself and other people.

Everything we do expresses what kind of a person we are. If someone goes into your kitchen to make a cup of tea and they leave the spoon on the floor, the tea bag dripping all over the counter, don't bother putting the milk back in the fridge, what does that tell you? It tells me that person is all over the place emotionally, that they don't know what they're doing, they're a mess, a walking disaster. It's about discipline and it filters down to every aspect of your being. When you're not in control of your emotions, believe me, your life has no order.

Until you control your emotional state, you'll find the same things keep coming up over and over. It's like the movie, *Groundhog Day.* The same stuff every day until you wake up to what's really going on.

Life is what *you* create and *you* have the power to change it any time you choose. Remember, it's your movie. You're in charge. You don't like it – start again. No one else can do it. There's no sense sitting around waiting for some guru to come along and give you the answers. You have to do it, go home to yourself, do the work, create the answers, be your own guru. You can't be lazy, slump in front of the telly night after night hoping the life you want is going to appear by magic, without you having to do anything.

Get cracking.
- Don't just sit there – do something.
- Bring about change, one step at a time.
- Be in control of your destiny.

Self-awareness gives you the knowledge and the means to make positive changes. No one is stuck with a life they don't want. The life you're living right now is the one you've chosen. If your home's chaotic, your relationships are always a mess, your job is making you stressed, you're eating and drinking too much and hating yourself for it, it's not because life's unfair – it's because you're not fulfilling your potential. You're not doing the work.

We *all* have freedom and choice. What we do with it really is up to us.

Change for the Better

Becoming more self-aware means your perception starts to change. Life looks different. It feels different. It is different. Once you're disciplined about leading a life that's ethical, caring and spiritual, balancing being selfless with self-care, you find that the negative stuff – obsessive behaviour, eating disorders, destructive addictions – has no power over you. You still hear the old man in the rocking chair, but he has a lot less to say and he's not controlling you anymore. You don't even listen to him most of the time.

The more work you do on yourself and the more spiritually in tune you become with whoever you pray to – God, the Divine, a Higher Power – the less the voice dominates. It's up against other, more positive voices telling you you're on the right track, that every day is bringing you closer to your goals, and that, actually, you're doing just fine.

Any time the old man gets loud it's a sign of self-neglect, a reminder you need to focus, get back in tune with your purpose, work on the spiritual side of your life. Take time out: pray, read something uplifting, feed your spirit with positive thoughts. It's not about going to church or being religious. It's about having a meaningful relationship with the Divine, in whatever way works for you.

I don't mind hearing what the old man in the rocking chair has to say anymore. I actually find him quite endearing because he serves as a reminder that we all have our fears and insecurities, and that they're just part of the human condition.

I'm so aware of how I used to be, how I'd listen to the old man, believe what he was telling me and disappear into a dark place. Now I think – 'How could I let those things mash me up?' We all do it, though, let the stupidest stuff mess up our whole programme because we let our emotional state spiral out of control. By doing the work on yourself, you stay in control.

Make the Time

It doesn't matter what else is going on in my life, how busy I am, I always make time to pray. I can get by without going to the gym for a week, but I can't get by without prayer. Before I go to bed I always have a talk with the man upstairs, read something spiritual or positive, maybe the Bible or some Sufi poetry – anything that's uplifting for the soul – and my spiritual connection is getting deeper every day.

There are times when I'm living my life at top speed, rushing about, multi-tasking, keeping plates spinning all over the place, and it's touching base

W